THE WAY TO LIGHT UP YOUR DIVINITY

A Dahnhak Master's Guide to
Human Perfection

Seung-Heun Lee

Dahn Publications
Dongil B/D 7F, 5, Soosong-Dong,
Chongro-Ku, Seoul 110-140, Korea
Tel: 82-2-722-7181, 91 Fax: 82-2-738-6167

ISBN 89-87293-06-8 03800

Cover painting: "Bell Rock" (1997)
"Bell Rock" was produced in Sedona, Arizona by Young-Ju Chang,
a Korean artist. He has been working actively in spreading and teaching
Dahnhak as Dahn Teacher Won-Am.

THE WAY TO LIGHT UP YOUR DIVINITY

A DAHNHAK MASTER'S GUIDE TO HUMAN PERFECTION

Seung-Heun Lee

dahn

TABLE OF CONTENTS

PREFACE

Throughout the history of humankind, various religious and spiritual traditions have sought the deliverance of human beings. Yet, the vast majority of people have not discovered the True Nature of their lives, and their souls are lost without finding any purpose in life. One of the reasons for that is probably an overabundance of thoughts and teachings.

Yet, I agreed to the publishing of this lecture series on Dahnhak because they are different from the existing teachings. My lectures, on the contrary, urge people to resolutely get out of the conventional mode of thoughts and religion.

A human being is the embodiment of the Law and Truth. To light up the True Nature of people enables us to get nearer to the Truth. I think the long-held belief about god needs to be changed, first. The god I have talked about in my lectures is not religious, but rather a principle and Law. The Law of the cosmos or the Principle of Harmony is the god I mean. We also need to let go of the learned ideas, thoughts, emotions which we have misguidedly believed as the true entity of ourselves.

In fact, no Truth can compare with that of "seek it in my body." Dahnhak is an art of training for body and mind which leads us to enlightenment through the wakeful gaze into the body. In Dahnhak, we try to understand Self and cosmos by understanding the working of Ki-energy in our body. We try to seek the Truth within our body because the Divinity is in each of us. But at the same time, Dahnhak Practitioners understand, "My body is not me, but is mine." Dahnhak encourages us not to be attached to our body but to be in tune with the harmony of the cosmos as a holistic human being.

I hope a number of people could realize the dire need for the field of "Human Perfection Science" after having read this book. I sincerely hope as well that people will reexamine their present purpose of life and sprout the seeds of seeking after Truth.

It seems that I have expressed some negative opinions about established religion. The current chaotic situation of the world has resulted not from the legal or administrative systems but from the foundation, root, and spirit. The Spirit of "New-Human/Harmonious-World" is magnificent, and I entrust it as the last spirit to save our global community in the twenty first century. A New Human is a person who is aware of interconnectedness between people. He or she not only joyfully walks towards the Physical and Spiritual Perfection but also willingly shares with and helps out others. When a lot of New Humans get together, their community naturally becomes a Harmonious World. Their culture is an enlightened one which is caring, accepting, trusting, free and creative. I sincerely hope the Spirit of "New-Human/Harmonious-World" can get the sympathy of many people in the world.

A good deal of my thoughts and hopes expressed in this book are not necessarily orthodox ones, and are short of completion. I wish those incomplete thoughts and hopes to be planted in the mind of the readers, and, in time, to grow and blossom into completion. Let us all become a New Human and join in the great work to harmonize human beings and all living beings.

May 10, 1999
Seung-Heun Lee

BEFORE YOU READ
THIS LECTURE SERIES

In *The Way to Light up Your Divinity*, Seung-Heun Lee presents Dahnhak from multiple dimensions and perspectives. He suggests how to develop the soul and raise the consciousness for people who are interested in spiritual growth. He freely speaks of practice, spiritual growth, Divinity and enlightenment. Sometimes he reaches down to an intimate detail on how he came upon enlightenment, and other times, he talks in a frank manner to his students as a teacher.

Though known to his students as Grand Master Lee, Seung-Heun Lee is mostly called "Seu-Seung" which means revered teacher in Korean. Compassionate and wise, yet so practical and down-to-earth, Seung-Heun Lee's spiritual guidance helps us arrive at peacefulness which springs up from realizing oneness by dissolving the separation between the Self and world, and the body and mind.

Lecture One, "Dahn-Jon Breathing for Healthier Body and Mind," was given to the public who had never been exposed to Dahnhak before. The rest of the lectures were given to the lifetime membership holders of Dahn Center.

In Dahnhak, the word *mind* means "the whole," integrating both reasoning mind and emotional heart. In fact, all the uses of *mind* in this book have been intended to mean whole mind, not a partial reasoning mind. *Mind* can also mean our inherent mind on which things are reflected as they are without being tarnished by our emotional states and outer influences.

The purpose of Dahnhak lies in both Human Perfection and Whole Perfection. Human Perfection has been expressed in ten different ways in this lecture series, and they are listed in the Appendix 4. Though different in words depending on which perspective is taken, those refer to the same thing ultimately.

The editing team would like to extend special thanks to Dahn Teacher In-Am for his help with clearer textual interpretations, and Camille Lirette and Allen Sutterfield for their help with clearer English expressions.

May 10, 1999
Editing team
Dahn Publications

DAHN-JON BREATHING FOR
HEALTHIER BODY AND MIND

Welcome to the lecture. I'm happy to be here to talk about Dahnhak with you. Dahnhak is a holistic health program which trains the body and mind. I'd like to talk about how to stay in good shape by spiritual practice without the aid of medicine.

Our body consists of the physical body, mind, and Ki-energy.[1] Between the body and mind there is an energy called Ki. Dahnhak systematically shows how to feel and make use of this Ki-energy. Ki is also called life force or bio-energy. In the old days few people experienced or understood this Ki. At present the practice called Dahn-Jon Breathing helps the participants to experience Ki with relative ease. As a result, Dahn-Jon Breathing is gaining popularity. Dahn-Jon is an energy center of our body which is located two inches below the navel and two inches underneath this point. Dahn-Jon Breathing is breathing not through our chest, which most of us are accustomed to, but

---

1) To learn more about Ki-energy consult Appendix 1.

through our abdomen. It will help if we imagine our lungs have been moved down to our abdomen.

Most people would think Dahnhak is the same as Dahn-Jon Breathing. But Dahn-Jon Breathing is just a program of Dahnhak Practice.

Let us begin with a simple exercise which will clearly show you how healthy and limber you are. Your current health condition and the level of tension in your muscles will be shown. So make yourself comfortable. Try not to memorize this exercise with your head, but rather get it with your body so it becomes a habit. Though brief, this exercise is designed to give you help in your day-to-day activities.

Put your hands together in front of your chest, palm to palm. Lock your fingers together. Now raise them over your head while twisting them so that palms can be up. Push them up further from the raised position once more. So far, this looks like a simple workout. Now we'll add breathing to this. Breathe in deeply, hold it, tighten your abdomen, raise your hands up as before, and then bring them down while breathing out through your mouth. One more time, breathe in, hold it, raise your hands up, push them up further, tighten your abdomen, bring them down and out goes your breath. When you compare the first workout with the second one integrated with breathing, you can tell the difference right away.

This exercise, making use of Dahn-Jon Breathing, is called the art of physical revitalization. It's to get our body working. There are over three hundred different ways to work our body in Dahnhak, but today I'll show you a few simple exercises which can be easily done in your office environment. On those afternoons when you are sleepy and tired, this exercise will pump the blood from your internal organs to all over your body, all the way to your extremities. The real difference between the simple workout and the one combined with breathing is that the latter amply supplies oxygen through the blood stream, and thus, relieves us of tiredness.

Another benefit of the exercise combined with Dahn-Jon Breathing is that the internal organs get moved up and down an inch or two, and blood supply to the organs increases. That's why, with Dahn-Jon Breathing, a noticeable improvement has been experienced by those who suffer kidney disorders, diabetes, various gastric diseases and neurosis.

There have been multiple analyses on the causes of this improvement in physical wellbeing. Modern medicine employs blood analysis. It has been shown that with Dahn-Jon Breathing, the blood circulation is quickened, the oxygen concentration in the blood stream is sufficiently augmented, and the blood itself is purified. Also, when we push and pull our muscles, our veins are elasticized. This stretching and contraction of the veins result in a decrease in cholesterol buildup.

The beneficial effect of Dahn-Jon Breathing can be explained on another level. One of the three Principles of Dahnhak Practice is WUFD: water energy up, fire energy down (Su-Seung-Hwa-Kang). It refers to the cold of water energy going up to the head, and the heat of fire energy coming down to the stomach. In cases of physical weakness or illness, our head is feverish. When we worry too much, a headache results because our head is inflamed with fire energy. But with Dahnhak Practice, our head gets clearer, and our abdomen gets warmer because the Ki-energy circulates, and causes the blood to circulate.

There is, however, one crucial element which affects balanced blood circulation. That is our emotions. Ill feelings trigger anger. Anger, then, directs the fire energy towards our head, which means that blood rushes to our head. But when we breathe through the Dahn-Jon, located two inches below the navel, the heat goes down toward the Dahn-Jon area. Dahn-Jon, which literally means "a field of energy," is an energy center. Many acupressure points are located around it so that the Dahn-Jon can function as a synthesizer and collector of Ki-energy.

In Oriental medicine a person needs a well-functioning blood circulation system and Ki-energy circulation system to stay healthy. Ki-energy collects at and passes through the 365 acupressure points throughout the human body. These acupressure points make meridian channels, the passageways of Ki-energy. Dahn-Jon works as a major storehouse and generator of Ki-energy.

Let me tell you a couple of problems which were overcome with Dahnhak Practice. I've seen those, with the eyesight in the range of 2 through 3 (partial blindness) even with their glasses on, improve their eyesight up to 15 (close to 20, perfect eyesight). Also, some people often find that their hands and feet are damp and cold. When they take part in an hourly Dahnhak exercise session once a day for three months, warmth will return to their hands and feet. This symptom may not be an illness but indicates a certain functional disability.

In other words, vigorous blood circulation leads to a clearer head and a warmer abdomen. Ki-energy circulation brings about blood circulation so even the most stagnant blood in the internal organs gets moved. The result is every part of our body functions better.

A cold abdomen area results from the opposite of WUFD. This can be the fundamental cause of our ill health. When some people readily have diarrhea after a glass of beer or a night's sleep without covering their stomach, that means they have cold internal organs in the abdomen. Dahn-Jon Breathing brings back clearer heads and warmer internal organs, and then saliva wells up in the mouth. Anxiety and restlessness result in a parched mouth and lower our body's self-healing power. While this condition persists, we are susceptible to contracting disease.

Too much strain on our nerves leads to overexertion which then results in illness. With Dahn-Jon Breathing, we have ample saliva welled up in our mouth, a clearer head, and a warmer abdomen. That is, our self-healing ability is maximized, which helps maintain our physical wellbeing. So the Principle of Health in Dahnhak Practice is that of

WUFD: water energy up, fire energy down (Su-Seung-Hwa-Kang).

But a demanding social life can often bring out just the opposite of this Principle. Heat rushes to our head when we use it too much. Then our abdomen always feels limp, and before long aging symptoms begin to accelerate. That's why it's important to keep our body in optimum health, and make WUFD a natural habit of our body for at least an hour a day by Dahnhak Practice.

Since breathing doesn't require any fitness machines, it can be done anywhere. Just quieten your consciousness, and breathe. The change in breathing habit will be a big help in keeping in shape. For those who suffer from chronic insomnia, Dahn-Jon Breathing can bring a wonderful relief. With Dahn-Jon Breathing, we can experience a transformation in which our physical constitution is changed.

Let's go back to our exercise. Our body tends to stiffen if not in use for a while. We'll lock our fingers in a different direction this time. Bring your right hand downward to the front of your abdomen. Turn it 180 degrees facing the palm outward. Now move your left hand towards it facing palm to palm, while crossing at the wrists. Lock your fingers. While inhaling, turn your hands inward toward your chest, and then extend them out away from your chest. Now hold your breath, and tighten your abdomen. Bring your hands back to their original position, and then exhale. Let's do it one more time. While inhaling, bring in locked fingers, and then out, hold your breath, and exhale. If you have difficulty with this exercise, the joints in your shoulders, elbows, and wrists are not limber enough. That is, your ligaments are too stiff.

This exercise with breathing stimulates the nerves and meridian channels, which in turn improves the function of the internal organs. Meridian channels are the passageways of Ki-energy in our body. Aging tends to shrink muscles. We are not aware of it in our daily lives because what we do mostly is just to sit around. So this sort of exercise is needed to check up on our muscles.

Let me show you another exercise to keep you in good shape. Put your feet apart about shoulder width, and then bend your waist and put your palms on the floor. You're supposed to be able to do this. When we are about sixty years old, we usually walk with our toes pointed outward. The reason is that our calf, hamstring and back muscles have shrunk. Then we feel cramp in our neck.

We should have stomach strength. The lack of stomach strength means no driving power to carry things through. You might have heard, "You have no strength in your stomach. Tighten it!" Without stomach strength our ideas just end up as ideas and never get translated into action. We use our head a bit too much.

Optimally the life expectancy of a human being is 120 years. Physiologically we have a body which can live up to 120 years. But our desires drive us to use our head too much and our body too carelessly, which results in 60 to 70 years of life at most. If we don't go overboard and maintain a well-balanced life, we're supposed to live 120 years and enjoy normal sexuality until 90. But in real life, we work our body too hard, paying no attention to it. When diseases or disorders break out, we go to the doctors to check it out. But without proper exercise, our body will become more dysfunctional.

Dahnhak fortifies stomach strength. Those who feel limp in their abdomen area have almost nothing to live on. Our abdomen should always be full and energetic. Everybody! Please stand up!

While carrying force in your abdomen, hit the area. When you get up in the morning, close your eyes, and hit your Dahn-Jon area about a hundred times. Face bright sunlight. If possible, don't face the wall. Hit your abdomen about a hundred times, and then, your blood will circulate vigorously throughout your whole body, and tiredness will be gone in no time. You'll feel an instant rise in the energy which have been waning. By hitting the Dahn-Jon area, you can't help putting force in the area. Without strength in your stomach, there's no strength in your lower back. Now, sit down, please! If you hear a sound like a drum and feel no discomfort when you hit your Dahn-Jon area even with your fists, then you can be assured of your good health.

I want to teach you one or two exercises and repeat them until you familiarize yourself to them. Let's start with usual breathing using our chest. Breathe in and out. Breathing can be divided into two methods. The first is breathing in and out through the nose, while the second is breathing in through the nose, and breathing out through the mouth.

Now let's get into Dahn-Jon Breathing. Straighten your back. With your back bent, there's no way your breath can reach down to your abdomen. Straighten your back, and put your hands on your abdomen. Breathe in. Think of it as an abdomen breathing. Breathe in, and push your breath down to your abdomen, and then breathe out. Imagine you have moved your lungs to your abdomen and nose to your back opposite of the navel. Don't force the breath. Just be natural with it.

In this exercise your face should be at ease, shoulders relaxed, and only your abdomen moving in and out. Never mind your nose. Just push out your stomach further away from your back, and then pull it in towards your back. While repeating, imagine the blood stored in your bowels flowing out to your veins and capillaries, and reaching out to every internal organ. Imagine this while breathing, then the breathing will become natural. Your stomach will be out with an inhalation, and in with an exhalation. So just push your stomach in and out, and the breathing will follow naturally.

I went to Mt. Song-Ri-San a while ago. An old monk named Sun-Am lives there. He's about 90 years old, and has been living on uncooked foods for about 40 years, which is only possible for an advanced spiritual practitioner. His hearing is still excellent, and he can read newspapers without glasses.

Some accomplished Dahnhak practitioners tend to stay away from the world. I wanted to seek out such people, and ask them to put our efforts together to make a much needed contribution to our society. That's why I visited Rev. Sun-Am in the heart of the mountain, but he denied his having practiced Dahnhak, even though he looked to be an accomplished Dahnhak Practitioner to my eyes. I understood he didn't want to be bothered. Outside he wore the robe of a Buddhist monk, but inside he was an accomplished Dahnhak Practitioner.

When our practice reaches a certain level, we can size up people with just one look at their eyes. When I saw the eyes of Rev. Sun-Am, I could see the advanced level of his practice, and asked him for shelter for the night. There were only two rooms, and one room was occupied by a woman, so I shared his room.

When the night advanced, I lay down, and pretended to be sleeping. At about four o'clock in the morning, he put his palms together in the lying-down posture. Then he rubbed them vigorously. Then he got up, and practiced for 20 minutes, which means he didn't breathe for about 20 minutes during which he circulated his inner Ki-energy one complete cycle. I found out then and there why he had excellent vision and hearing in spite of his old age. When we put this into practice, it will surely improve our health. So I'll show you how to do it. This exercise is best done in the morning right after you get up.

Rub your palms vigorously. Not a simple rub, but a rub while holding your breath. Rubbing your palms while holding your breath draws the inner Ki-energy of your body outward. Your palms will get warm instantaneously. Put your warm hands over your eyes. Also, while your palms are warm, pass them over your face three times. After three times your palms won't be warm anymore. Then rub them again. Put them over your eyes. Next, turn your eyes clockwise about ten times. Leave your palms as they are over your eyes, and just turn your eyes. And then turn your eyes counterclockwise about ten times. Then take the palms off the eyes.

Rub your palms again to get them warm. When they are warm enough, put them over your eyes again. This time move your eyes upward as far as possible, and downward as far as possible. Repeat this. When your palms get cold, rub them again and put them over your eyes. This time move your eyes to the left as much as possible and to the right as much as possible. Repeat this. This is how you improve your vision.

Rev. Sun-Am turned 90 but still maintains his youthful looks. He doesn't use soap or toothpaste. He washes his face as if he's massaging it. He uses cold water even in Winter. Next, rub the skin around your eyes clockwise, and then counterclockwise. Next, rub over the back of your neck. Next, with your middle fingers, rub the sides of your nose, which will make your face look healthier and more resilient. Next, rub the joint connecting your upper and lower jawbones.

Rub your palms again. Sweep over your ears. I'll show you how to improve your hearing. Cover your middle finger with your index finger. Then put them on the flat surface, and let the index finger hit the surface. When you look at the back of your ears, you'll see bones protruding. Put your middle finger covered with index finger over those bones, and hit them with your index finger. Make a loud noise, and let your eardrums resound with the noise. This will strengthen the nerve cells inside the eardrums. Hit them the number of your age.

The sound should be as loud as that of a drum. This concludes the simple exercises to be done when you get up in the morning: the exercises of eyes, ears, and face including the pulling, pushing, and hitting procedure. Next, stand up, bend forward, and touch the floor with your palms. Repeat this about ten to fifteen times. All theses can be done in 20 minutes.

Next, make Dahn-Jon Breathing a part of your life during the day. I mean always breathe not through your chest, but through your stomach. Stagnant blood is always present in the stomach. When we pump it out to receive a fresh supply of oxygen, our health can be improved. No medicine can do this as effectively.

DAHN-JON BREATHING IS A PART OF DAHNHAK PROGRAM

These days Dahn-Jon Breathing is known to almost everybody in Korea. Also, Dahnhak has come to the knowledge of many people. I've been asked a number of questions about the relationship between Dahnhak and Dahn-Jon Breathing. So I'd like to clarify a few points now.

Dahnhak and Dahn-Jon Breathing share a common element in that both require an understanding of Ki-energy. Dahnhak is, like Dahn-Jon Breathing, a practice to understand Ki through our body. The Dahn-Jon is located about two inches beneath the navel. In Oriental medicine, it is called the Ocean-of-Ki-energy point, which means it is the reservoir of abundant Ki. Dahn-Jon Breathing is breathing through the Dahn-Jon.

All living beings breathe. Those who don't know Dahn-Jon Breathing breathe through their chests. So it is said that small people breathe through their throat, and big people breathe through their soles.[2]

---

2) To learn more about Sole Respiration, consult Appendix 3.

When we breathe through our throat, it is usually when we are weak, extremely angry or on the verge of death. Another expression is "one is gasping for breath." Some breathe through their chests, and others breathe through their Dahn-Jon.

In Dahn-Jon Breathing, there is a procedure to master and accumulate Ki-energy. Dahn-Jon Breathing is a program of Dahnhak Practice and also, the breathing method for the beginning practitioners. In Dahnhak, we do Dahn-Jon Breathing until we activate and complete the Girdle Meridian Channel (Dae-Mak). This channel is located around the waist, beginning from the navel about where we put our belt on. After we activate Dae-Mak, the next step to follow is circulating Ki-energy through the Conception Meridian Channel (Im-Mak) and the Governor Meridian Channel (Doc-Mak).[3] The breathing method in this step is Skin Respiration.

Have you ever seen a snake breathing? A snake breathes with its whole body. Its body gets larger and smaller with each breath. No wonder a snake enjoys such longevity, and never becomes ill. In comparison with its body size, no other animal can put forth the same strength as a snake. It can exert an enormous power compared to its weight because it breathes through its skin. When we incorporate Skin Respiration as part of our daily breathing, we are said

---

3) Consult Appendix 7 for the diagram of three important meridian channels.

to have achieved the Microcosmic Energy Circuit. When we reach the Microcosmic Energy Circuit, we can completely circulate Ki-energy throughout our body, including the Conception and Governor Meridian Channels, the Eight Mysterious Meridian Channels, and all of the Twelve Symmetrical Meridian Channels. This can be called the intermediate level in Dahnhak Practice.

At the advanced level is the Sole Respiration. Breathing is carried out mostly through the acupressure points on the soles of our feet. In Sole Respiration, our astral body can be outside our physical body. In other words, we can enter and exit our body of our own will. When we incorporate Sole Respiration as part of our daily breathing, we are said to have achieved Macrocosmic Energy Circuit, in which we become one with the Cosmic Energy. Cosmic Energy is the energy of harmonious cosmos and also the highest level of energy.

Achieving the Macrocosmic Energy Circuit is called Supreme Enlightenment in Buddhism and AESA (Attaining Enlightenment and Sharing this Awareness with others) in Dahnhak; first, we attain enlightenment, meaning our True Nature merges into Cosmic True Nature and second, we actively share this awareness with others. It means we are at home with the True Nature of all things. To summarize, Dahnhak Practice has three steps: Dahn-Jon Breathing, Skin Respiration, and Sole Respiration.

But to reach Skin Respiration, we need to be free from desires and learned conceptions. So to be able to enter the state of Skin Respiration requires the purification of the mind first. Then we can enter the world of enlightenment. Dahnhak can help us accomplish the state of enlightenment.

Recently I see many Buddhist monks and nuns coming to the Dahn Centers. There's a saying that Koreans have a secret key to enlightenment which was passed down from their ancestors, and that is Dahnhak. Enlightenment is too ambiguous and hard to grasp. We only understand it as a rigid conception. Dahnhak presents enlightenment systematically and shows how our body changes when we reach a state of genuine enlightenment.

A while ago a college student came to me and asked me to teach him the art of cultivating the ability to get to places fast. He said he would quit school after he had mastered the art. So I asked him why he'd bother to learn that when he could take the airplane with just a little money. He said he just wanted to give it a try because he wished it from the bottom of his heart. Modern science has already accomplished all these: the ability to get to places fast (planes, buses, trains, so on), second sight (TV), hearing the sound of far-away places (phones), seeing through the walls (X-ray). It's just a waste of time to try all these when science already provided these.

Dahnhak has its purpose in accomplishing what hasn't been completely successful in religion and philosophy; to restore physical and spiritual health for an individual and to establish an enlightened culture for the humanity. Material revolution has been completed, but spiritual revolution is yet to come.

Dahnhak shows us "my body is not me, but is mine." We need to be the master of ourselves. We can't do any harm to our body when it is ours. When we are fully aware that "my body is mine," we feel like we have an automatic control attached in our body that when we think it's harmful to our body, our body naturally rejects things like liquor, cigarettes, or gambling.

On the other hand, even though we think that's terrible for our body, and want to quit, our old habit may still dictate to our body. This is like driving a broken car. Our body not under our control is like a "broken car." Dahnhak helps us realize "my body is not me, but is mine" and allows us to be in control of our body. Most people today are under the control of their body, though. We need to be able to subdue the desires of our body. In reality, however, we live a life just to fulfill our desires. So we falter in the swamp of desires for a brief moment, and soon our last day comes.

Think carefully if you're in control over your body or controlled by your body. We are controlled by our body when we are too busy meeting the needs of our palate, eyes, ears, and desires. When we are in control over our body, then we are the master making use of our body of servant. When we are in command of our body, we have our right spirit intact. When we are controlled by our body, our spirit is gone.

The cravings of our body know no limit. Serving the master whose desires are endless leaves us confused. We are nervous and restless. That's why our times are called the era of lost Self and why so many people have ailing hearts. Too much fire energy in the chest leads us to lose peace and suffer emotional instability. Even a trifle can trigger our anxiety and pounding heart. We blow up for nothing, feel insecure for no apparent reason, and our mind finds no peace. All these have the root in the fact that our spirit, the right master of us, doesn't do its job but serves as a servant.

Our body gets comfortable, we have an occupation and honor, we've made money; yet our mind stays unfulfilled. Our mind suffers further when its body contracts a disease. To make it worse, if mind has to serve a body with no honor, no job, and no money, the pain becomes unbearable. When we are on top of our greed, we get to rule it. It means the Heaven and Earth are back in their right places.

In the old days, a doctor could see the whole body of a patient. But modern medicine has specialized fields according to the parts of the human body, and doctors cannot examine the whole body anymore. Examining only the ears doesn't mean examining the person. When we cut a potato and keep cutting it, we reach a molecule and further down an atom. At this level, it's no more a potato.

Too much analysis can lead to losing the real thing and result in chaos. We have lost the real meaning of the very existence of the religion, art, and medicine. Most of us know something's wrong in this world, but we don't know what's right. By not knowing what's right, we have no way to correct it.

The root cause of all these problems is not in the law or systems but in the foundation, roots, and spirit of people. Without sound spirit, only thoughts and knowledge abound. Thoughts and knowledge without a proper foundation of sound spirit can only serve as servants of lust.

Dahnhak doesn't seek something big but intends to get our right spirit back. This spirit resides in our body. Therefore, it can't be found in the Bible, Buddhist scripture, or an ethics textbook. We need to find it in our own body. That's why we breathe mindfully, to get our spirit back.

We need to make the purpose of our breathing clear. Because we've lost our master, our body is ill. When we get our right spirit back, the impure energy in our body runs away. Suppose you left your house without locking it, and then come back in about a month. What do you think you'll find? You'll find all kinds of people in your house. Because our spirit is not in its right place, those unwelcomed guests like disc disease, stomach disorders, or headache make themselves at home in our body, posing as our masters.

In Dahnhak, to have the mastery of Ki-energy is to become friends with our body. We regain our spirit and then, regain our mind. This mind is an inherent mind which allows us to see things as they are without being tarnished by our changing emotions and outside influences. To see the True Nature of our mind is AESA; attaining enlightenment and sharing this awareness with others.

Thus, in addition to Dahn-Jon Breathing, Dahnhak has a philosophy, the core of the Truth. After we get our mind back, we begin to genuinely enjoy our lives. To appreciate the aesthetic way of life is not easy. Those who live an aesthetic lifestyle are hard to find in modern times, but in the old days they were called Cosmic Beings, meaning they hold Heaven and Earth with their lives. They have realized the ultimate oneness of Heaven, Earth and Humans. They are unconstrained in coming and going. They are not bound. When Cosmic Beings do things for others, they don't get attached to the fact that they have done good deeds for others. They are like water. They do things, rejoice for the good result itself, and leave. They are no different from saints and sages.

According to Korean traditional philosophy, the saints and sages were not ones of high standing. They all lived an aesthetic way of life. Many aspects of these people should be redefined. When we get our Ki-energy and mind back, the aesthetic way will come naturally from within ourselves. We need to find the purpose of life and get our spirit and mind back.

[4] *Let me tell you how we can get our mind back. This is from my personal experience of practice. I heard when we regulated our inner Ki-energy, we'd become unparallelled in physical strength. So I started on a kind of martial art, and then tried another. But*

---

4) Grand Master Lee's personal practice experience is presented in different font to distinguish it from the main text on Dahnhak.

nothing worked, nor did anybody teach me how to regulate the inner Ki.

But in the midst of my wandering around, I found one common element. Ki-energy is not to learn, but to experience through our body. How do we experience it? Just keep looking at our body mindfully, sort of like meditation.

I am neither a Christian nor a Buddhist. So I can't possibly say I meditated. I just sat in the snow-covered field, straightened my back, evened out my breath, and looked into my body. Then, all of a sudden, a surge of heat passed through my body, and I felt hot all over. It was a bitter-cold winter day, about one degree Fahrenheit, and I had sat over there for about three hours. I had entered into the state of Non-Self. Later I found the snow where I had sat all melted away.

It was then and there that I felt an enormous power within my body. I circulated this Ki through hands and feet. I realized I can make my body either warm or cold depending on my mind. That's how I found out that my body is mine, and it can become mine through Ki-energy.

After this experience, I wanted to learn the True Nature of this thing that regulated Ki and controlled my mind. So I entered Mt. Mo-Ak-San and resolutely

---

5) Cosmic Mind is the Principle of Harmony and the Principle of the cosmos. Cosmic Mind is the originator of Cosmic Energy.

began to practice. I realized, then, "My energy is Cos-
mic Energy, and my mind is Cosmic Mind."[5]

Then, I became free from my body. All those ques-
tions I had held in my mind were answered, and I
became free from all desires. After that I considered
myself a rich man. Everything in the world was Cosmic
Energy and Cosmic Mind, and therefore, everything in
the world was mine.

Next, I was able to make use of the thought energy.
Normally a thought is just a thought. After I practiced
Dahnhak, I was able to use my thought energy. Thought
energy can even kill a person. When we receive Cosmic
Energy through Dahn-Jon Breathing, our thought ener-
gy can be amplified. That's how I was able to open up
eleven Dahn Centers all over South Korea in the begin-
ning. Now, the number has increased to 360 Dahn Cen-
ters throughout the world.

In Dahnhak, each of the numbers from one to ten has a
symbolic meaning. For example, ten symbolizes perfection,
and nine means chaos. At the moment, I think the world is in
the state of number nine which is very chaotic. Everybody
thinks he or she is the best. The next number from nine is
ten. Ten is the very number of harmony, perfection, and
Truth. Furthermore, the number ten in Chinese word (十) is
the same as the symbol of Christianity. Both of these sym-
bolize Truth. When we put this ten inside the square, it
becomes a word as in Dahn-Jon (田). Dahn means Ki-energy

and Jon means a field. So Dahn-Jon means a field of Ki-energy.

The number ten symbolizes harmony. The cosmos was created through the harmony of the Heaven and Earth. All things in life are produced out of the harmony of the cosmic dual forces, Yin and Yang. Earth and female are considered Yin, while Heaven and male are considered Yang.

We almost arrived at the state of number ten. There is, however, a possibility to go back to zero instead to ten. We are in a critical situation. Going back to zero means the explosion of the planet earth. So right now, we have two ways to go: zero or ten.

So those are considered crazy who claim they are the best. Now's the time to say, "You and I are not two but one" or "We have to unite to survive." Those who harmonize with others are respected, while those who are domineering will be shunned.

I see many young people in the crowd today. I want you to listen up. Looking at college students around me, including my own brother and nephew, makes my heart ache. They have no idea how lucky they are to be born at this time. They are lost because nobody showed them the right way. Facing the best times which come only once in five thousand years, what would you do? We have only one life in this physical world. What would you do? What you need to do is to create a new world. When you make this your vision and mission, I'll let you know how to do it.

This work is not to be done by myself. I could open up

eleven new Dahn Centers not by some political power or through financial supporters, but only through my conviction and sincere help of my students. Dahn Centers are different from other martial arts or health centers in that Dahn Centers are non-profit organizations. It all started when eight people with the same aspiration got together and collected their lifetime membership fees. The first Dahn Center was born that way, and soon, more and more people got involved.

Dahnhak has been accepted as part of a curriculum in the Military Academy. At first the Military Academy employed a different practice. But the students complained that the practice didn't work, or they were not interested at all. So the administration ordered to close up the class. At this point someone suggested to try Dahn-Jon Breathing. So the Academy sent out three professors to check up all kinds of Dahn-Jon Breathing places in the nation for two months. They thought the most crucial thing is neither the techniques nor the methods, but the spirit in practice. So the professors carefully compared the way of practice among many different disciplines and chose Dahnhak.

They held the spirit of Dahnhak superior. A person inside the Academy told me that the spirit was clearly alive in Dahnhak, and the masters in all Dahn Centers put in all their efforts to their work. Dahnhak is practiced at schools, too. A while ago over 200 professors in Kang-Won University had a Dahnhak retreat for four days. In addition, many high schools have Dahnhak Practice session once a week. Students experience better concentration and sustaining power.

To operate our body, our mind should be connected to the Ki-energy and Spiritual Energy. When those connections are cut off, our body operates just as a body, while our mind operates just as a mind, and there is no connection in between: We drag around our ill-functioning body and naturally get into confrontations with others. Fights are breaking out all over. Weapons are wielded. There's no senior or junior.

In this turmoil, some seem to think all things and all people should perish in an instant. This is an extreme thought. When so many people say it's better to die out, we'll actually die out. On the other hand, when a number of people say things will work out, they will really work out.

We shouldn't just sit around and wait for good times to come. Even when the spring comes, those who haven't prepared the seeds to sow cannot embrace the coming Spring. Only those, who have prepared, sowed, and grown seeds, can reap the harvest in the Fall. So we need to prepare our own seeds.

To be able to prepare seeds, we need to first get our right spirit back. Next, we can sow the seeds of our right spirit all over the world. Be prepared to receive the seed of Cosmic Being, in which Heaven and Earth become one. The difference between Dahnhak and Dahn-Jon Breathing lies right here, to have this seed of Cosmic Being or not; Dahnhak not only restores the health of mind and body for an individual but also recovers wholesome caring spirit for our neighbors.

In the past, to appreciate and experience Ki was really difficult. But Dahnhak has made it easier. My purpose lies not in teaching the techniques but in helping you understand your True Nature. I'm generous in teaching techniques because I don't want to make money out of it. Because techniques take time to learn, however, I teach them little by little, but you can take home a whole year's learning of Dahnhak today in this place. It all depends on your wholeheartedness. In fact the techniques are only an instrument to let you feel and experience Ki-energy. What's critical is to get our spirit back.

THE PROPER ATTITUDE OF THE
DAHNHAK PRACTITIONER

For Dahnhak Practitioners, the mental attitude before embarking on the practice is crucial. Some want physical wellbeing, while others want spiritual growth and eventually want to attain the enlightenment.

The purpose of Dahnhak is AESA; attaining enlightenment and sharing this awareness with others. It means a person not only lives a life with an enlightened consciousness but also tries to share this higher consciousness with others. While doing so, the person naturally builds enlightened culture around himself or herself. Usually people take Dahnhak Practice to stay healthy. But once they achieve optimum health, many of them move on to acquire spiritual wellbeing. Some take Dahnhak Practice to attain enlightenment from the beginning. They have the right purpose to practice, but they are so few.

The white uniform we wear at the beginning of our practice symbolizes the clearing of our desires and emptying of our minds. We need to empty our minds. If we come to the Center just with desires, no matter how great a Cosmic

Energy pours in, it only inflates the desires.

To give you an idea of what the emptying of the mind is and how crucial the emptying of the mind is in the spiritual growth, I'd like to tell you about the ten-year learning of the Way in the old days. When the students first knocked the door of a hermitage of a teacher in search of the enlightenment, they didn't get any teaching right away. Instead, to give the students a chance for emptying their mind, they were made to work in the kitchen for three years. But many of them left in the middle because they had to work in the kitchen for so long without getting even a bit of teaching.

In a sense, working in the kitchen without payment could be considered a kind of punishment to some people. But rendering services like that was considered to show the student's resolution to practice. After that, another three years were dedicated for collecting firewood. Only those who survived this hardship of six years were given the chance to learn and practice.

But in our times people pout their mouths with great dissatisfaction even for a free work of a month or two, let alone a year. All sorts of negative words are uttered such as they were taken advantage of or they sacrifice too much. Those people wouldn't learn much even if the teacher appeased them into the teaching.

To prepare meals in the kitchen was a service for the teacher and a courtesy. The students put in their labor, and offered a meal to the teacher. The teacher didn't even provide the rice in some cases. When there was no rice, the student was still supposed to offer a meal even from begging. When the students collected firewood, they were not supposed to cut just any wood. In the same way they cut away the undesirable aspects within themselves, they had to cut out only the bad branches. So they cut wood with a mind to groom themselves. Cutting a well-grown branch had to be avoided at all cost. When they cut only the bad, perished, wilted branches and put them into the furnace, they were learning to put their desires and impurities on fire.

After six years had passed with this work, finally the teacher passed on the teachings and practice. But those who hadn't emptied themselves yet even at this point had to repeat the process of preparing meals and collecting firewood. For three years, the teacher passed on the teaching. The remainder of a year was passed doing self-trial. So this was called a ten-year learning: six years of cooking and collecting firewood to prepare for learning, and four years of actual learning in which the preparation period was longer than the actual learning period.

I've been looking for people since I began spreading Dahnhak. But I don't deny the desires of people. So for those who have illnesses, I teach how to get better. But that's not my real intention. The desires of people have no end. That's why they say an ocean can be filled up, but not the desires of people.

What I sincerely want to tell you from the bottom of my heart is about the True Nature of a human being, the potential of every living being.

On our path to the Way, health is important. But too many have their final destination on health, living only to satisfy their body. But the body we train, polish, and serve with too much trouble is perishing and dying out with time. Most of us live to please the eyes, ears, tongues, or thoughts, but the real master of us is not one of these. The true entity of us is not like that.

We are bound by time and space. It is our human nature to want to fulfill our desires faster and in a bigger way by any means. This is the war against the time and space. The war over how fast we can do it, how much more we can do it than others, and how much more we can eat and possess.

Most of us live for ourselves. But each of us seems to perceive the width of Self a little differently. For the sake of Human Perfection, we need to deny ourselves for once. An exhaustive self-examination will reveal our True Self. In the midst of out-and-out self-examination, we cleanse out all the accumulated impurities again and again. When there's nothing to wipe out, the True Nature of people will reveal itself.

When we learn things and make them ours, our True Nature is covered more with those things. So this Practice is doing it in reverse; unlearning, so to speak. The learning of the world is to acquire and accumulate in our brain and body. In the learning of Dahnhak we cleanse out and throw away. Only after repeated cleansing, are we ready to receive the Way of Heaven. But as long as we hold on to the desires, even the best teachings can't penetrate through us.

The white uniform you are wearing now is the purest.

As we proceed on to the higher level, we'll find more to cleanse out. The more we progress, the more we need to wipe out. That way, in the end, we become bright like a light.

In Dahnhak, we need to learn to love our body. Without the love for our body, we're not capable of loving others. That is, blind practice wouldn't lead us to the enlightenment. After learning to love our body, we can become a New Human, an individual broadly benefitting other beings, and then we can build a Harmonious World. This "New-Human/Harmonious-World" is the purpose of life for every Dahnhak Practitioner.

To be a New Human, we need to have a healthy body. When we are ill, we become a burden to everyone around us. So we need to have a proper diet. To live by the nature of things begins from myself. The beginning of world peace starts from me, from how much I put into practice the Spirit of "New-Human/Harmonious-World" and how much I live my life in tune with the nature of things. When you eat, stay away from overeating or selective eating, but rather eat proper amount of a balanced diet. When you sleep, have a deep rest. In doing so, we can feel not only the energy in our body but also the energy of the cosmos.

For this Practice, we need to compose ourselves. That's why we're wearing a white uniform. The learning of the world will produce greater success the more we want out of it. But the learning of Dahnhak requires emptying of the mind.

Grateful attitude is also crucial. We have so much to be thankful for. But we never seem to express enough appreciation. Our heart's continuous pounding doesn't owe it to us. We're not the master of our heart. In fact we don't know when it might stop. It could even stop while we're sleeping.

Is there any one of you who has come out into this world out of your own efforts? We were born without any hard work on our part. We didn't sign up a contract with the Heaven when we were born. Nobody signed under the terms that he or she will live 80 or so years. In Dahnhak Practice, when we open up our eyes in the morning, we are thankful that our eyes are opened again. We become humble that much. We are thankful we could open our eyes this morning, and our heart is pounding even now. Nothing beneficial will come out when we keep complaining like "I'm short of that, I don't have enough of that."

We need to stop rushing about. Why are you in such a rush? We've come to this world, and ultimately we'll all go away from this world. What is there to rush about? When you breathe, even out your breath. Breathe in and out slowly, and compose yourself restoring tranquility. Nothing is to be rushed. When you rush, does the globe turn faster? Do you know why the world enjoys such a long life? Because it turns regularly. The sun comes up exactly in the morning, and goes down precisely in the evening. It never puts itself in frenzied haste or the race against clock.

Only people rush about. All we need is three meals a day, a place to sleep, and work to do. But we rush things way too much. I want you to look back on your life while walking with an even stride without being distracted by the surroundings. Then serenity and composure will spring out from the depth of you. That way our heart will be tranquil, our liver will be calm, and everything will get composed. When you become a billionaire or receive a great honor, will you be praised by the Way which has sent you to this world, like "wow, you're great"?

This planet we live on is nothing but a tiny bead floating around in the cosmos. Compared to that, how big do you think your existence is? No matter how splendid your work may be, it's insignificant. So I urge you to slow down just one beat in your walking. Then you'll be genuinely rich, rich in heart.

You may say I have an illusion, but I think this whole world is mine. Not only in my mind but in reality it is mine. I can see things whenever I want to and go places wherever suits myself. It may not be mine on official papers but am I inconvenienced in any way? I pay the admission fee, put up a tent, sleep a few nights and come back. Who could interfere with me? If I were the owner, I would have to pay taxes. If I were the official owner of Yellowstone National Park, I would have to pay a huge sum of tax to the State. The fact is that the State takes care of everything, and I go there once or twice a year paying an admission fee. How economical!

What's important is that we have three hearty meals a day, draw up our energy, and take care of things one by one neither too fast nor too slow. Then enjoy the nature of things while doing so. I live by the Way I was born with and feel satisfaction from the heart. Everything visible or tangible changes. Don't rely on these.

Live a given life wholeheartedly, and work on things you set your heart on with all your might. You'll find the Way in doing so. The Way doesn't reside in faraway places. Some say they don't feel anything particular or haven't changed a bit after they took up Dahnhak Practice. They feel that way because they haven't emptied their minds.

Consistent practice brings in peace, and that's good enough. We keep practice so as not to be shaken of that peacefulness. Once we go out to the world, our inner life is shaken again. That's why we need to come back to the Center to recover tranquility. Get a grip on yourself and praise yourself like "okay, you're doing excellent. You're living in tune with the nature, and that's all that counts." In case you don't live in tune with the cosmos, then you need to do some soul-searching. This is the basic purpose of Dahn Center. It's not for learning more things.

To feel that there's a change or no change indicates the practitioners brought in the habits of the world with them. Try to have the mental attitude like "that's great" or "I'm peaceful." You are here to regain your innate True Self which is always peaceful and composed. You are here to give a break to the restlessness resulting from everyday life. Here you breathe quietly, get your serenity back, and keep your mental state well-balanced.

When our inner center is connected through the Heaven

and Earth, we are in the state of individual enlightenment. It is similar in the way that male and female are united. Male and female are united not because someone taught them how to do so. Likewise, individual enlightenment is not to be learned but to be felt like "this must be it," while living in tune with the nature of things. When we are awakened to the Truth of the cosmos like "this is the way to live a life in this world," we are no more bound by the concept of time and space. We'll be aware that life and death are nothing but an illusion, life is the gate to the death, and death is the gate to life. Going back to the innate True Self, the Self before we were born, is Human Perfection. Since this life is given to us, it is natural for us to live with zeal. But the concept of living with zeal is distorted. Many assume living faster is living with zeal.

I'd rather use the word "well" than "with zeal." Living well will do. So everybody says to the students to study "with zeal," and the students naturally think only the first place is acceptable as a token of studying with zeal. "With zeal" means getting in the heat of passion.

To say "Live well!" doesn't give us a burden, but to say "Live with zeal!" feels burdensome. That's why I keep saying "Do it well, doing well is enough. Staying around middle is good enough!" Living well is all we need. Dahnhak is not to be done with zeal. Just breathe in and out well. Like the wave that comes and goes, breathe well.

The Consciousness of the Dahnhak Practitioner:

Inner Consciousness and the Unconscious

For Dahnhak Practitioners, the level of consciousness on which their practice is based is a crucial factor. Dahnhak is a field of science, and therefore, to study the theory is important. The levels of consciousness are divided into three: outer consciousness, inner consciousness, and the unconscious. The analysis of brain waves by EEG gives us a clearer idea. Outer consciousness is in beta state which has the brain waves of 13 Cycles per second and over. Inner consciousness is divided into two which are alpha state of 8 to 12 Cycles per second and theta state of 4 to 8 Cycles. The unconscious is in delta state which has brain waves of below 4 Cycles per second. The unconscious or delta state means Cosmic Consciousness.

Those who entered the state of the unconscious are called saints. Books, too, are written in outer consciousness, inner consciousness, or the unconscious. The Bible and Buddhist scriptures were written in the unconscious. In the state of the unconscious, we can say, "You and I are one, I am the god, or I created this world."

Freud compared the world of the unconscious to an iceberg saying the outer consciousness is no more than the tip of an iceberg. The enlightened one is no more religious. Awakening comes not from learning, but from practice. The great saints didn't attain enlightenment out of learning. Rather they went through spiritual practice, the practice to enter the state of the unconscious. Only one out of a million people are capable of this: a task as difficult as a worm turning into a butterfly.

The outer consciousness is known to everybody, but the world of the unconscious is unknown. The Self in the outer consciousness is small and narrow-minded. It's not the Great Self. The awakened can freely go in and out of the world of outer consciousness, inner consciousness, and the unconscious. They have solved all problems about the spiritual world. In the state of the unconscious, if someone cut off our arm, we wouldn't be aware of it.

Usually people have brain waves of over 12 Cycles per second which is beta state. A writer or painter usually stays around 10 to 12 Cycles which is alpha state. Artists sometimes experiences a flash of inspiration rise up spontaneously: this is possible because they are in alpha state. Jin-Dong, the shaking of body which is sometimes experienced by Dahnhak Practitioners is possible below 12 Cycles per second. Twelve Cycles and under can be called a state of sleep or deep relaxation in which we can see things if we want it with all our heart. At this time, if color vision appears, we are in the theta state which means deeper relaxation than the alpha state of black and white vision. If the Goddess of Mercy appears during our practice, it means we're in a state of inner consciousness which is alpha or theta state.

Basically there are two causes of dream. The first is to release the repressed desires, and the second is to foresee what's going to happen in the future. To dream to release the suppressed desires serves the same function as to speak ill of someone in higher standing behind their backs. This is not to blame. Through dreams we can get into inner consciousness. In the world of inner consciousness, even the fall from the cliff leaves us less injured. The same is true of an insane person who doesn't get sick from scavenging in the trash cans. A shaman doesn't bleed from dancing on the edge of a sword. Many things which could go wrong in the outer consciousness turn out all right in the inner consciousness.

Among the dreams to predict the future are the death of the state head, outbreak of war, and death of a family member. An unusual sensing ability is exerted in the inner consciousness, which the outer consciousness isn't capable of. That's why so many accounts of dreams appear in the Bible and other scriptures.

People usually get into inner consciousness unknowingly, but the advanced practitioners get into the state of inner consciousness with their awareness present. During Dahnhak Practice, most practitioners are in their inner consciousness. Sometimes, they see visions, but they're not sure if the visions are real or an illusion. Once they're in the state of the unconscious, they can distinguish between the real and the illusion. From this time on, they're never bound by anything.

A novice practitioner can't tell the difference between a real image and a virtual image. In the same way, shamans claim the deity they've seen is the highest. They're playing the video the way they want for their own interests. The same is true of a dream. Some of our dreams are better than reality. When we hear that it's not real, we get upset. Especially when we are in a sweet dream, the person who wakes us up looks so detestable.

None of this happens in the world of the unconscious. The world of the unconscious is neither suggestion nor a revelation. The unconscious comes to us as a concrete sensation. For example, to our mind comes a consciousness that you and I are one. Then, we realize all of us come from one root, and the concept of life and death disappears. The question of life and death is, then, solved. The shortcomings of the inner consciousness are that only one aspect or limited aspects of things are seen. This is overcome in the unconscious, and eventually a consciousness that "I am you" and "you are me" slips in, and then, we can see all around, the whole 360 degrees. This is Cosmic Consciousness.

So many religious leaders talk of revelations. But great saints didn't talk about revelations. They just talked of compassion, mercy, love and benevolence. "Love your enemy" can only be said from the unconscious because enemy doesn't exist in the world of the unconscious. Suppose while you're sharpening your pencil, your right hand cuts your left hand. Would you chop your right hand off? Your right hand and left hand are from one root. The unconscious is at the true entity.

All beings rest in the world of the unconscious. Looking from the unconscious, the saying of Jesus in the Bible that "I am the road, Truth, and life. Those who carry heavy load come to me. I will give you rest in me" didn't mean Jesus had lots of money or buildings. Rather, he said it to himself like a monologue from the state of the unconscious. This is called the Law. It just comes out without any preparation.

The articles of association of Han Cultural Institute Corporation include the development of spiritual guides. The essential quality of the spiritual guides is to be at home with matters of the mind. The unconscious is hard to be seen or proven. Boundless unconditional love springs out from the unconscious.

When Jesus said, "I existed before Moses, even before Abraham," many laughed and mocked that it didn't make any sense. Jesus also mentioned, "I was on the right of the Lord before the creation of the cosmos at the Genesis." The Korean sage Jeung-San said, "I am the Heaven. I am the moon and the sun." All these came from the unconscious. Things ordinary people wouldn't understand are uttered in the state of the unconscious like "great sound is no sound and great light is no light."

Dahnhak has its roots in the Dahn Life Words, "Cosmic Energy is my energy, My energy is Cosmic Energy, Cosmic

Mind is my mind, My mind is Cosmic Mind." This is the alpha and omega of Dahnhak propagation. Dahnhak is just the tools employed to teach this. This is the world of my consciousness, True Nature of cosmos, and the mind of cosmos. Seen from the unconscious, the world is so perfect that nothing needs to be changed. To the ordinary eye, however, it's overflowing with things that should be changed.

People always tend to see this world as an incomplete one. Some people start a revolution justifying themselves that it's for the benefit of the people. From the enlightened point of view, this world, when left alone, will change itself when the time comes. Those who are born at the right time will read the current situation and come forward in the name of a people or nation. They can just feel the trend in the air.

In fact, those who started a revolution acted not for the people but for themselves. It is true that Jesus and the Buddha lived for others, but at the same time they lived for themselves. In helping others they found joy. They chose the life of helping others because they found joy in that lifestyle. That's why we can say Jesus and the Buddha lived for themselves. But seen from the outer consciousness, it doesn't look that way.

I was reading the column in a religious newspaper and it was written that the offenders of the sexual torture incident, the death of a college student from torture, and the kidnapping of a little girl all believed in religion. On the question of "character building comes first or faith comes first," more emphasis on the faith will rather produce selfish believers. They care for Jesus or the Buddha rather than their fellow humans.

The education about inner consciousness is needed now. Lectures wouldn't be a proper medium for this education. Inner consciousness is very sensitive. When a teacher talks of moral uprightness but acts in a way that gives a special favor to students whose parents gave him or her some monetary gifts, it actually engraves in the heart of students that moral education just serves the purpose of passing the test at school, and the reality is that money talks. For, inner consciousness gets the message not through words but through images and Ki-energy. That's why Dahnhak Practice is one of the best media for the education of the inner consciousness.

Our society needs good images. We need to make the time for soul searching. Reflect on our wrong consciousness while breathing. Our habit belongs to the inner consciousness. For example, when we try to quit smoking, though our outer consciousness acts out behaviors like cutting out the cigarettes, if our inner consciousness wants them, quitting is impossible. But Dahnhak Practice can send a message directly to our inner consciousness, letting it realize the unwholesome consequences of smoking such as cancer and addiction. When we smoke after that, our body shows some rejection symptoms like nausea. If we always run away on seeing dogs, we have a deeply engraved fear of dogs in our inner consciousness. Preconceived fear is rooted deep inside. Running away from dogs means our inner consciousness is controlled by our outer consciousness.

When we size up people well, we have a well-developed inner consciousness; we're aware of them through intuition and images. This is called an extrasensory perception. Continued spiritual practice develops our inner consciousness. The unconscious is Cosmic Consciousness. Seen from the unconscious, this world is perfect. When the business owner looks like an exploiter and the worker the exploited, it's seen only from the outer consciousness. This is supposed to change even if left alone. Just like we will change our posture when one leg goes asleep.

The ultimate purpose of our practice is to peacefully stay in the unconscious. Inner consciousness can be reached through our dreams. Dreams are often correct because many of them appear in a detached mind regardless of being harmful or wholesome. But the inner consciousness while being wakeful can be tarnished by personal desires, and then it can be correct only one out of hundred times.

The absence of desires is the world of the unconscious, but inner consciousness can be caught in greed even in dreams. Joy and fear all arise from selfishness because we are attached to the notion of "I." When there's no Self, there's no joy, no fear. The Self disappears, and then, no more life or death. The greatly awakened has no mind. The greatly awakened, like Heaven, has no heart, but creates all beings, and yet doesn't show any pride in doing so.

About the way to be enlightened, I gave you all the knowledge at the moment we met. But I teach you with the desire to spread Dahnhak and you learn this with some desires, too. What we need to seek is the consciousness free from desires.

When we give Ki-energy to someone, there should be a cause for us to feel like giving it. This cause is the same as the saying, "You reap what you sow." The Law is only passed on through mysterious causality. Ki-energy is the sound from our heart. The desire to give Ki to someone comes from the unconscious.

COMPLETE HEALTH COMES FROM THE LIT-UP TRUE NATURE

Dahnhak consists of several developmental steps, but with an open mind those steps are not as important. Dahnhak isn't just composed of lectures to give knowledge. It is also a procedure to observe what's happening in our body. To know the inner consciousness, and further on, the unconscious is not something we can learn, but rather something we should see, to be more exact. This state of consciousness is also called "to be enlightened" or "awakened."

Our ordinary eyes can't see the inner consciousness. We need to have eyes which are capable of seeing it. So to be able to understand my lecture, you need to wish for the eyes that can see the inner consciousness. Though we have eyes, they're not trained to see the world of inner consciousness.

People have outer consciousness, inner consciousness, and the unconscious. Outer consciousness wears masks and pretense. When nobody's around, we easily slip into our inner consciousness. There, we take off our clothes, sing out loud sometimes, or speak ill of our parents. But we can't even dream of doing these in our outer consciousness. Moral education should be intended for the inner consciousness.

Dahnhak is a study of the inner world. When we wear the uniform and sit for the practice, all kinds of thoughts arise. In the midst of the seemingly endless stream of thinking that comes and goes, we get to ask ourselves: "Why are all these thoughts arising, especially those negative thoughts? Am I really this negative a person? Can't I think of something clearer and purer?"

After going through this inner conversation with ourselves for about two months, we'll find ourselves begin to be cleared of many dissatisfying problems with ourselves and everyday life that have occupied our inner consciousness. We will become quieter and clearer. A lot of negative thoughts and information we have accumulated from our daily lives will be cleansed. Dahnhak makes it possible. When we wash the dirty clothes, we first grasp them and then let go of them; in this way, we repeat rubbing and kneading. Likewise, when we repeat breathing in and out, Ki-energy and blood circulate better, and with that, the impurities of our inner world go out from our body.

Dahn-Jon Breathing is one of the best ways to get rid of all those distracting thoughts. When a lot of impurities from the inner world go out, pure thoughts will naturally come up. When habits are changed, the change in the character and physical constitution naturally follows. The practitioners purify themselves towards the Way. Until we get to our True Nature and Divinity, we need to keep cleansing away the piled impurities inside. It's not like embellishing with something new but rather like wiping away and polishing.

Some people are good at criticism. They have accumulated a pile of impurities in their inner consciousness. When there are some problems, we find three kinds of people in the ways to solve them. The first kind works the problems out discreetly not letting others know, the second kind makes them worse, and the third kind calls out a big crowd to lay claim to his or her achievement. Many people belong to the third kind. A big person works things out quietly and enjoys the inner satisfaction of it while a small person wants to get back exactly what he or she has put into.

Those who hold lifetime membership in Dahnhak can be said to take the course of spiritual leadership, and they should put their purpose of life in Human Perfection. We need to polish our inner consciousness and make it sparkle like a diamond.

Dahnhak is a practice to be purified while breathing. Dahnhak Practitioners have clear and bright faces. Those who have scowling faces are full of complaints and dissatisfactions. They keep complaining everywhere. They know no happiness even when faced with fortunate events. They are releasing darkness from within their inner world. This kind of people makes even the cleanest environment darker. But those with a bright and right inner world light up their surroundings.

The purpose of Human Perfection is to illuminate the True Nature of Self. To illuminate our True Nature means to become one with the Way.

We contract illness because we are not in tune with the nature of things. With our True Nature uncovered, we can enjoy health. This Practice aims at healthier body and mind for an individual, and further on healthier family, society, and humanity. When our True Self brightly sparkles, we will experience an utmost joy and bliss. When the health of life itself reaches the highest, many fundamental problems of human existence will be solved such as the problem of life and death, that of rich and poor, and that of right and wrong. And with that, our True Nature will brighten up further.

Those with their True Nature lit up are harmonious people. They make things well not only for themselves but for others. Koreans have the spirit of "that's great!" When we say "that's great," our shoulders naturally dance up and down, while our mood is changed accordingly. To be good is to be opened. We need to say, "that's great" in the morning and evening. Words have power in them.

Those who easily contract illnesses often say "that's terrible" and surround themselves with impure atmosphere. Even the stomach disorder gets better when we keep saying excitedly "that's great" for about an hour. When we say "that's great," it really becomes great, and when we say "that's terrible," it really becomes terrible. Those who studied Ki-energy will understand this easily. We need to stimulate our Ki by saying "that's great" as often as possible. When our Ki is enlivened, our illness is gone.

But we shouldn't say "that's great" when we do something bad to others. "that's great" encompasses being good to others as well as to ourselves. Korean ancestors said "that's terrible" when harm is done to others, and "that's great" when good is done to others. Based on the spirit of "New-Human," individual broadly benefitting other beings, the expression of "that's great" was uttered from the point of view of others.

Close your eyes and imagine something good. Imagine something you can do that can make others happy. When we say "that's great" and imagine something good, a good energy will spring up from our body. Then most of our bad inner consciousness will be gone. Our dark face will be brightened, and the tone of our skin will change.

Say "that's great" and circulate Ki-energy throughout your body; imagine something good while enlivening Ki by dancing shoulders up and down. Then our wish can be firmly engraved in our inner consciousness, and soon, it can come true. Right now I'm imagining that Dahnhak is spreading all over the world, and all people in the world are saying "that's great!"

The beginning of our body started with our parents, but that of our mind is further before that in time. The beginning of us is Physical Energy, a material essence. Nobody has seen the beginning of Physical Energy. This cosmos was created out of True Nature, but in time the True Nature disappeared, and desires rule the world. We need to open the world of True Nature again. When we are in control of mind, we are in control of everything.

It is my opinion that there are ten kinds of break-throughs. By breakthrough I mean something that was considered impossible due to human limitations has become possible. Nine out of ten of them have already been accomplished, and only the last breakthrough has yet to come. The last breakthrough is that of the spirit, and thus, only the spiritual revolution has yet to come. For example, the vision breakthrough (TV), sound breakthrough (phone), transportation breakthrough (plane), second sight breakthrough (x-ray), language breakthrough (translating machine), season breakthrough (fruits and vegetables in Winter) have all been accomplished.

Ours is the time to enjoy the prosperous material civilization. If only the spiritual breakthrough was here, our world would be complete. Let us put our efforts together to make this spiritual revolution possible. Dahnhak is here to help with the spiritual revolution.

Our True Nature is complete in itself and doesn't feel uncomfortable even without the legs, arms or internal organs. Inside ourselves lies the True Nature with no beginning and no end. True Nature sparkles radiantly. When we take a good look into it, we will realize True Nature is a real thing. When we become one with our True Nature, the distinction between "life and death" or "you and I" disappears. The True Nature can be divided into thousands or tens of thousands, but still, at the root, is one.

THE WAY TO TRUTH IS
WITHIN MY BODY

The Truth is inherently one. Then, what is Truth and since when has it been here? It was here before human beings were born. The Truth can be called the Law of Nature. When the Law of Nature came into being is unknown. But there's one thing the saints agree upon, and that is "Truth has no end." Even at this present moment, all beings are living in the Law of Nature. We live a life by the creating force of nature.

Those, who were awakened to the Truth and talked about it, didn't even bother to make religions. They just passed their awakening to the disciples. But the disciples got together, formed an organization, and after some time, when there was a difference in opinions, they formed some new sects of religion. When the masters taught, they didn't teach the doctrines or methods, but rather taught the Truth itself because they were the ones who recovered the senses to feel the Truth. But those people who listened to these masters heard them as the doctrines and methods. That led to the trifling difference in opinions. It's common knowledge that

Christianity has over forty religious sects. The situation is not much different in Buddhism. I am a man of religion, but definitely not a man of a sect. I think everybody is a person of religion.

An atheist believes in the religion of "there is no god." A theist believes in the religion of "there is god." Within the boundary of "there is god," there are many branches and sects. A religion teaches the Truth, and therefore, all people can get out of religion. It all comes down to one question: Is there a god or not?

I'm telling you about Ki-energy. When the words come out of my mouth, they're not about the methods. But you listen to them as methods. I tell you to concentrate on your hands if you want to feel Ki because where there's mind, there's Ki. Ki-energy can take the form of electricity but at the same time, the cold, the humid, and the cool are all Ki. The taste is Ki, too. The taste of sweet, hot, bitter and salty, all of which are Ki. The light is Ki-energy and so is the dark. All of you feel Ki. The Ki I'm talking about is life force, which an ordinary person won't be able to feel unless he or she is concentrated.

Ki is present in both you and me. If you want to feel this Ki, you need to concentrate. It's like when I want to understand someone, I need to turn an attentive ear to this person. If I'm watching a movie while this person is talking, I can't understand this person. It's true that Ki is inside my body, but if I am distracted, I can't feel this energy within myself.

So it is said, wherever mind goes, Ki-energy flows. The mind not only taps Cosmic Energy but also creates energy. With concentration, Ki is accumulated, and when enough Ki-energy is condensed, vital life elements such as blood and Physical Energy are strengthened.

Buddhism talks of our mind like "everything depends on my mind," or "There is neither a beginning nor an end in the cosmos." Christianity talks of God. Confucianism talks of Ki-energy in *I Ching*. Dahnhak talks of Physical Energy, Emotional Energy and Spiritual Energy.[6]

With the cultivation of Physical Energy, purified Emotional Energy comes, leading to brightened Spiritual Energy.

Among the developmental steps of Dahnhak Practice according to Ki-energy use, the first step is to feel and understand Ki-energy. The next step is to accumulate it enough, and then, proceed on to circulate it through Dae-Mak (Girdle Meridian Channel), Im-Mak (Conception Meridian Channel), and Doc-Mak (Governor Meridian Channel) and finally put it into circulation through all the channels of the body. When we have accomplished these, we have achieved the Microcosmic Energy Circuit. That concludes the development of the body, and the next step is the development of mind. That's why Dahnhak is called an integrated field of study. Steady Dahnhak Practice heals illness and brings wellness back. So it is therapeutic. With steady

---

6) To learn more about Physical Energy, Emotional Energy, and Spiritual Energy, consult Appendix 2.

practice, our head clears up, and we'll get to be aware that "my body is not me, but is mine."

To understand Ki-energy, we need to focus our mind on our body. The Buddha said, "You can't attain the Way even with all the money in the world if you seek it outside your body." Another saint mentioned that attaining Way is simpler than touching your nose while washing your face.

Then how come the Way, that is supposed to be so easy to attain, is so hard to get in reality? It is because we're trying to touch our nose while we are scratching our buttocks, so to speak. We think the texts have Ki, Spiritual Energy, and the Way. In fact, texts are only paper and ink.

To get an understanding of our mind, we need to seek it within our body. The same is true of understanding the Spiritual Energy. Jesus said, "I am in your body and you are in my body." Now we can easily find one thing in common from these saints: we need to study and practice while putting our body at the center. Socrates said, "Know thyself." Confucius said, "All the Laws reside in your body. You are a miniature of the cosmos."

For example, as the planet earth has continents and oceans, so we have internal organs. As the earth has trees, so we have hairs. As the earth has mountains and rocks, so we have skin and bones. As the earth has running rivers, so we have Conception and Governor Meridian Channels (Im-Mak and Doc-Mak). As the earth has oceans, so we have hearts. As the earth has streams, so we have capillaries. A year is made up of twelve months, and our body Twelve Symmetrical Meridian Channels. A year has 365 days, and our body 365 energy points or acupressure points. We can see we are the microcosm or mimi-cosmos.

Genesis says that a person is made to bear a resemblance to God. God in Christianity is omnipresent, that is, dwelling everywhere. The appearance of God is that of cosmos and of people as well.

The difference between the religion and Dahnhak lies in that Dahnhak seeks Truth in the body while religion tries to learn it through the religious texts or doctrines. When we hold on to the doctrines which are nothing but tools to teach the Truth, we become too much attached to them, and then we can't turn our attention to our body.

Scriptures can be compared to microphones. When you study by listening directly to the teacher, it is like turning an attentive ear to our body, and that is Dahnhak. All scriptures are a kind of teachings, and the means to get to the Truth, but they are not the Truth itself. The awakened can feel the Truth. When this is translated into words and letters, they get to lose the heart and soul of the Truth.

All people want to seek the Truth, an eternal life, and the Way. The passageways to these are within our body. What makes our heart beat? The energy of nature keeps working through our body. It is our body that holds life.

LET US POLISH UP THE ESSENTIALS, NOT THE ACCESSORIES

Let us think about the intrinsic qualities today. There are the essentials which are the inner core, and the accessories which are the outer shell. But we cannot tell the essentials from the accessories. The interest on the intrinsic has almost disappeared and few fields of study teach the intrinsic. Actually, the scholarship tends to serve the purpose of teaching the peripheral or accessories.

We seem to pay great attention to accessories. The examples are too many: knowledge, thoughts, views on religion, ideas, money which we cherish the most, honor, power, clothes, and foods. These things have their value in their function to cultivate the inner core.

We are likely to think of spirit as an idea. But it is not. On the contrary, the spirit is the inner core. One of the three Principles of Dahnhak is PEA-EEP-SEL; Once Physical Energy accumulates, then Emotional Energy becomes pure, and then Spiritual Energy lights up (Jong-Chung, Ki-Jang, Shin-Myong). Physical Energy is a real thing, not an idea in our head. We want our Physical Energy filled up, our Emotional Energy purified, and Spiritual Energy lit up.

There is Emotional Energy between Physical Energy and Spiritual Energy. That's why Physical Energy comes before Spiritual Energy. Physical Energy doesn't move, but Spiritual Energy is mobile and bright. Though they say that death comes from the blockage of Ki-energy, they never say Physical Energy is stopped up. It is said that one has Physical Energy or one doesn't. Spiritual Energy is never said to be stopped up either. It is either bright or dark.

To express the inner core and True Nature, the knowledge, philosophy, idea, ideology, and religion are needed. We have lost our intrinsic spirit. We live day by day with little awareness on what our spirit is. Dahnhak is a practice to regain our spirit. We usually think of spirit as a concept, not as an inner core.

Many people don't live for the essential but for the money and fame. Money, fame and power exist to uncover the inner core or True Nature. They are needed to some extent to reveal our True Nature, but overindulgence in them subordinates ourselves to them. In the mean time, our True Self loses the place of the master, being debased into a servant.

Dahnhak is practiced to regain our spirit. It's a lonely way. It's often said that the sense of honor wouldn't feed people. They say all matters are directly connected to bread. But the matter of basic human needs, which are food, shelter, and clothing, has been solved in most areas of the world. Dahn Centers have come forward to seek the True Nature of people and have striven diligently to let this True Nature be known far and wide.

People are precious in this aspect of True Nature. When we cast True Nature away, we have nothing to cherish. We are of value in spirit and True Nature. Animals also have Physical Energy, but not the spirit people have. Animals have Ki-energy, too. Their Ki is mighty. Ki keeps developing and becomes Spiritual Energy, but animals' Spiritual Energy is, though not absent, too lowly in nature to evolve into higher Spiritual Energy. Ki-energy is not considered valuable based on its strength. As of strength itself, a bull or an elephant would be one of the best. What matters is where the level of one's Spiritual Energy is: to be an animal or a person, that's the matter of concern.

In the final level of Dahnhak Practice, the practitioner knows the True Nature of things. The practitioner awakens to the true entity, which is supreme enlightenment. It has nothing to do with the fact that Girdle Meridian Channel (Dae-Mak) is activated or Conception Meridian Channel (Im-Mak) is awakened. Those are nothing but the result of the activation of Ki-energy. It's irrelevant from "entering of the stars into my head." Now close your eyes and listen to this.

It was one dark night
Suddenly plunged into my head
one brilliant star
and whispered to my ears

The glittering stars in the sky are seen
because your eyes are seeing them
the rain beating against the windows is heard
not that you are hearing them
but that your ears are hearing them
I thought it was I who looked at the stars
and listened to the rain beating against the window
But now with my eyes and ears open
I realize I am the stars and rain
Oh, the brilliant light shines once more
and I realize I am neither the starlight nor the
raindrops
Now that I understand all
and am awakened to my True Nature
words are too shabby to convey this
Outside the window in the sky
still glittering are the stars
and endlessly falling down is rain.

The purpose of Dahnhak Practice is first, PEA-EEP-SEL; Once Physical Energy accumulates, then Emotional Energy becomes pure, and then Spiritual Energy lights up (Jong-Chung, Ki-Jang, Shin-Myong). Second, we get to see the world of brightened Spiritual Energy, and through that, we are able to meet with all beings at the level of True Nature. Only then, can my inner core be illuminated through the interaction with the inner core of the other person.

I urge you to keep communicating with Heaven to

make your True Nature sparkle. The level of Ki is varied for each person. Also, Ki is ever flowing in and out of our body. Physical Energy can be filled up, but ill maintenance of it causes the rapid drainage, too. Therefore, we should take good care of our Ki-energy. To fill up the Physical Energy, we just need to eat, sleep, and breathe well. The terrestrial energy combines with our breath, producing Physical Energy.

The key to the purified Ki is purified spirit. However strong our Ki-energy may be, if our thought is impure, our Ki would be impure leading to its bad use. So don't take pride in powerful Ki. It's enough for us to remain active. The real concern is how to refine it. For it is Spiritual Energy that directs us. Our Spiritual Energy should be shining ever so brightly.

When we have a pure, sparkling spirit, Ki is naturally built up. Then strong Ki out of emptied mind will surround our body. When there is a core, Ki-energy will naturally encompass the core. Therefore, what counts is if we have the core or not.

We are supposed to realize this by ourselves, but to put it into words in spite of the shortcomings of words, it will come to this: We need to seek for and cultivate the True Nature. We need to free ourselves from our accustomed conceptions.

This is no time for sticking only to the breathing. This is not to say that building up Physical Energy isn't important. In fact, proper breathing comes to us naturally in time.

It's not something we can force upon ourselves. Rather, we need to take a good hold of our spirit. Letting go of it means letting go of the Energy Line. The Energy Line is a figurative line that connects our inner center with the Cosmic Mind. It can be compared to an umbilical cord when we are in the womb of Mother cosmos.

The True Nature of our life is unchanging. I urge you to keep in mind that you live forever according to the Law of Conservation of Mass. Nothing gives me more joy than to discover that I have an eternal life. It is rejoicing to the utmost. Our physical body is just an outer shell. To know what's not changing, what's enduring forever, is most important.

The pure and beautiful will inherently go up, while the impure and heavy will sink down to earth. We can see the rain when the clouds turn into rain and come down, but we can't see the vapor when the water in the ground vaporizes and goes up. So to be seen or unseen is an uncertain thing. To be more exact, what is seen is innately what is not seen, while what is not seen is innately what is seen.

This is all due to the limitations or illusions of our eyes, but, if a supernatural sight is given, we could definitely see the vapor going up. But, in reality, only the falling rain is seen. The matter of how to connect the inner core with outer shell comes up again; how to connect the True Nature with preconceived notions, the invisible with the visible. We need to see the eternally unchanging inner core.

I AM A COSMIC BEING

A Cosmic Being is one who is united with Heaven and Earth. He or she has realized the ultimate oneness of Heaven, Earth and human. With the opening of Dahn Centers, *Cosmic Being* was published a long while ago. But I have waited for the right moment to come, and today I can give you a lecture on it. This is the theory and principle of Dahn-hak.

This book, *Cosmic Being*, holds all the principles on the cosmos and human life. This is an invaluable opportunity for you. I want you to listen up with reverence and an open heart.

A Cosmic Being is one who opens up a new Heaven and a new Earth. This world has an old Heaven and an old Earth at the moment. It is colored with corruption. Our physical body is invaded by illnesses and our mind by various worldly desires. As a result, regardless of the learned or the ignorant, people are confused as to what is right living and what will become of them tomorrow. We lost our balance, drifting and wandering about.

Plants take root in the Earth. People have their roots inside. When we take a look at the lungs in our body, they have numerous roots. Plants die when their roots are cut off, and so do people when their lungs stop. They can live without limbs but they die when they can't breathe due to a disorder in the lungs.

Therefore, the roots of people look like they are extended toward the body, but actually they aren't. These roots of people don't get the nutrition from the body but from the Void or Heaven. So roots are hidden within the body, but, in reality, the roots are spread deep into the Void. The Void is the spring of life.

We make an idle living without being aware of this Principle of Life. We need to understand the preciousness of Heaven. We need to be mindful of the fact that we are a part of nature; however, we have disregarded nature. We don't adapt ourselves to the nature, but rather try to dominate it. While keeping up with those tendencies, we have brought about the destruction of nature, being distressed with the consequences.

From a small perspective, we seem to control nature. But when we cut away a hill and make a sports field, or if we walk on the moon, are we controlling the moon or hill? Boundless arrogance has caused people to suffer the consequences. The Spirit of Cosmic Being is not to control nature but to make harmony with it. The Spirit of Cosmic Being is founded upon the oneness of Heaven, Earth and human. Because human and Heaven are one, and human and Earth are one, humans naturally want to make harmony with all people and all beings in the universe. We have lost the Spirit of Harmony and lived under the notion that we should control things.

A Cosmic Being has a thorough understanding that people are just a small part of nature. He or she is not arrogant but humble. When people make some money or come to fame, they are likely to become arrogant, and this is the time their sickness sets in. Their destiny is bound to go downhill from then on.

Although the humankind has seemingly developed outwardly, it has walked a corruptive path continually, and can be said to be failing at the moment. We have turned in the wrong direction. Change of direction is inevitable. And the change should be brought in at once by someone who is well aware of the Principle of Harmony. The Principle of "Live and let live" is the Principle of Harmony.

The human body gets sick when it loses the harmony. In other words, when the heart is too strong and the stomach is too weak, or when the liver is strong and the kidneys are weak, the body has no choice but to get sick. The concept of harmony is not established in our mind yet. So we need a training. When we incorporate the Spirit of Harmony, we can become a Cosmic Being by whom a new Heaven and new Earth will be opened.

Listen to these Dahn Life Words.

Cosmic Energy is my energy,

My energy is Cosmic Energy
Cosmic Mind is my mind,
My mind is Cosmic Mind

Numerous spiritual practices have led me to awaken to these words. With these, I have spread Dahnhak. I didn't learn Dahnhak from anyone. These Life Words are at the very core of my awakening. I realized I and Heaven are one.

Those who haven't experienced Ki-energy will find it hard to perceive. Ever since I first began to experience Ki, I had practiced it for the sole purpose of discovering the identity of this energy; where it came from, and how old it was. After I became aware of the real nature of Ki, I realized that this energy was Cosmic Energy and Cosmic Energy was my energy. Also, spiritual practitioners say, "mind, mind" and I was wondering what this mind was, and how my mind was different from Cosmic Mind. After some practice, I got to know that my mind is one with Cosmic Mind. Therefore, your mind and my mind are one, too. Though thoughts are different, mind is one. Form is different, but the ultimate reality is one.

One of the three Principles of Dahnhak Practice says, "Where there is mind, there is Ki-energy, then blood and Physical Energy are strengthened." (Shim-Ki-Hyol-Jong) When we concentrate our mind on our palms, we can feel

Ki-energy there. For, Ki goes to where our mind goes. Again, where there is mind, there is Ki-energy. When enough Ki-energy is accumulated, blood and Physical Energy are strengthened. The origin of everything is the mind.

We often say we can't live without love. When our Physical Energy amply accumulates in the Lower Dahn-Jon, love naturally springs up. The very reason the moral education in schools has failed is that they teach without love. Government designated the sixteenth day of May Teacher's Day, and took other measures to let students have appreciation towards their teachers to no avail. Students hold no respect for their teachers because there is no love between them.

Education without love can't be said to be an education. Technical education is possible without love, but true human education can't be done without love. Then who should carry out this human education? Nobody but parents, who hold true love for their children, can do the job. Parents of today, however, expect teachers will do everything, including human education. They are gravely wrong. Human education will be at its best when it is carried out by parents through love.

The kind of education I'm carrying out at this moment, also, will be most effective if it is received with love through Ki-energy. Otherwise, there's no meaning. When you and I are connected by Ki-energy, you will be one with me through love. With the help of Ki, you will understand that your Ki and my Ki are one. Those who feel the presence of love between them and me can get good learning out of this lecture. The moment we can't feel any love towards someone, a great wall will be erected which significantly disturbs our ability to learn and communicate.

So before you take this class, try to open up your mind and feel the love between us. I give you this lecture with love, and then it can be passed on to your heart, leading to communication between you and me.

Among the Dahn Life Words, one says, "We are One Grain in One Enclosure under One Divinity." Divinity is the Cosmic Mind and True Nature of life. One Divinity is the Cosmic Divinity. Divinity is like a seed. A person has a person's Divinity and Heaven has Heaven's Divinity. The largest Divinity of all is One Divinity.

Here, the word, "we" includes not only people but also all living beings and nature. The "enclosure" is symbolic of a fence in the cosmos. But from a small perspective, our body can be an enclosure and so can a pig pen. Even a cell membrane can be an enclosure. But from a large perspective, enclosure means the very cosmos.

We are One Grain in One Enclosure under One Divinity. We are One Grain: not separate, but connected with one another. The concept of "you" or "I" is an illusion, and a way of classification used for the convenience of living. Grains are separated. From a point of view of an ordinary person, you and I can be separated, but from the point of view of a Cosmic Being, all beings have their roots in Heaven and therefore are called "we." Taking roots in Heaven, we get nutrition from Heaven.

Heaven and Earth are one inherently, but people separated them. Intrinsically the True Nature of all things is one. When we clearly realize this, we'll understand the concept of "you and I are one." We'll get to see the true entity of things. We'll also get to see it is the words made by people that separate things.

Heaven and Earth look separate, but are connected as one. Where can we draw a line to separate one from the other? Earth holds numerous Heavens. From outside it looks all solid and blocked, but in the depth of the Earth, water is flowing. Water is made up of particles and atoms. Inside atoms, there is plenty of empty space: voidness is the nature of Heaven. On the other hand, everything is Earth. In the air, there are many elements from the Earth like carbon, hydrogen, and so on. They are not seen by our eyes, though. Modern science has developed enough to give us an understanding of this. It's scientifically validated. But in the old days, when an awakened spoke so, we had to just believe.

Among the Dahn Life Words, one says, "My body is not me, but is mine." Only those who know what "me" means can say this. This cosmos is mine too. This is the voice of the Divinity. Then, I am One Divinity, and this One Divinity resides in my head and sacred Cosmic Energy is steeped in my body and limbs.

If we understand this, we can say we have learned the real meaning of the following Dahn Life Words: "I am a Cosmic Being," "I am Cosmic Energy," and "I am Cosmic Mind."

THE MOST PRECIOUS TREASURE IS OUR DIVINITY

Today, I'd like to tell you about a precious treasure. This treasure won't change even after thousands or tens of thousands years have passed. If we find the treasure, all our problems will be solved. We can get all we want. This kind of treasure is within our body.

If we don't know about it, it's like we are not aware that we have a treasure of tremendous value in our own house. The treasure can't be seen or touched. But all things in this world, if seen by our eyes, are supposed to change. Things visible are of vanity. They are not to be relied on.

When the love between a man and a woman inflames, they think the love will last forever, but it lasts just a moment. When we come to fame, we think the fame will be with us eternally, but that, too, is only a moment. Everything changes. Our body changes too.

But there's one thing that won't change forever. The eternally unchanging is precious. The reason treasures are valuable is that they don't change. Things changeable are not treasures. The least changeable in quality is a diamond.

That's why a diamond is invaluable.

But we have something more precious than a diamond within us. I spread Dahnhak just to let you know that. The name of that treasure is Divinity. Only people have it. We have to unearth the treasure named Divinity. It means we have the qualities of god in our body. It's not at some far-away place, but rather within our body. This Divinity is One Divinity.

"One Divinity resides in my head and sacred Cosmic Energy is steeped in my body and limbs." The Divinity hasn't changed but is covered with multiple layers of block-ages because of our desires and lust. If we polish these blockages off, we can have everything. True happiness can-not be acquired from outside. It lies in the depth of our heart. How moving to know that Divinity is within us! Since our Divinity is not bright enough, we suffer from physical illness and mental loneliness. Because our Divinity is not shining, we have greed and have taken wrong actions. We live an insecure life in the fear of death. The answer to this is not knowledge. Divinity doesn't reveal itself if we become a Ph.D, achieve higher learning, or have a high intelligence.

When we make a resolution to light up our Divinity, we can live for the eternally unchanging. When our mind lights up, we can find our Divinity. This Divinity will give us peacefulness and sacred energy. We will be aware that infi-nite energy surrounds us. When the Divinity is revealed from within our body, sacred energy will be steeped in our body.

We practice Dahnhak to accumulate Physical Energy,

then to purify Emotional Energy, and then to light up Spiritual Energy. The Divinity is our True Nature, and thus, we should attain the dazzling radiance of our True Nature. Divinity is who we are inherently.

The True Nature of us is our Divinity. There is a fundamental difference between the one who tells their children from infancy that they have something precious in their body, which is called Divinity, and the other who lets his or her children just eat delicacies and live a comfortable life. Their directions of life will be greatly different. We need to spread to this world that we have Divinity within us. You have the mission to pass this on to those around you as I have passed it on to you.

COMPLETE HAPPINESS COMES FROM SATISFYING OUR DIVINITY

Everybody lives to become happy. All people, the lowly or the noble, a man or a woman, the learned or the ignorant, live for happiness. To be happy, we need to have physical wellness and then, based on that, build our spiritual wellness, too. Happiness cannot be a whole with the satisfaction of only the material needs like food, clothing, and shelter. They could be the basic conditions to become happy, but what's truly important is how we satisfy our Divinity. So complete happiness comes from both physical and spiritual wellness.

Happiness in a narrow sense lies in satisfying the desire to possess. I've been satisfying the desire to possess, too. I've striven hard to satisfy this desire to possess. In addition to me, the Buddha, Confucius, Jesus, and Socrates satisfied their desire to possess. They could grow physically because they satisfied the desire to possess. Had they disregarded this desire to possess early in their lives, they couldn't have grown. But even when we satisfy the desire to possess, there's a limit to physical growth. Our physical body grows only to a certain limit.

Most people put in effort to satisfy their desire to possess for happiness. There's no such thing as sin in this world if seen from the perspective of a vast cosmos. Seen from the mind of an immense Heaven, everybody is living zestfully for life and satisfying their desire to possess. It is beautiful. Depending on time and place, or the ground to see it from, it can be said to be good or evil, but fundamentally there is no virtue or vice. From a large perspective, everybody is living with wholeheartedness and zest. Even gangsters or con-men rob and con people with all their heart. Of course it's not fair to the victims, but still, from a large perspective, they are living energetically.

One's sensation and level of consciousness are not perfect. We often have our physical checkup. We have the standards of wellness to apply to our body to decide if it's healthy or not. But we have no standards to apply to our mind to decide if it is sound or not. As a result, endless chaos, fighting, and strife go on. It's like someone trying to build a house without a definite plan. We need to have concrete standards to define what happiness is so we can seek happiness.

In Dahnhak, happiness comes from wellness. Complete wellness comes from physical wellness and spiritual wellness. For spiritual wellness, we need to cultivate our Divinity and eventually merge our Divinity with the Cosmic Divinity. To become one with the Cosmic Divinity is called Human Perfection in Dahnhak. So complete happiness comes from Human Perfection. When our Self melts away and fuses into the Cosmic Divinity, we feel an indescribable rapture coming from a higher dimension of consciousness. Also, because all living beings are interconnected and no living being can exist without the cooperation of other living beings even for a moment, we naturally want to extend and spread this joy as far as possible. So true happiness comes when all beings in this world are happy.

Where does this health come from? It comes from rightness. To distinguish what's right or wrong comes from knowing the principles. Health has its own principles. In Dahnhak, the Principle of Health includes that of WUFD; water energy up, fire energy down (Su-Seung-Hwa-Kang), and that of PEA-EEP-SEL; Once Physical Energy accumulates, then, Emotional Energy becomes pure, and then, Spiritual Energy lights up (Jong-Chung, Ki-Jang, Shin-Myong). Problems arise when we move away from these principles.

For example, according to the Principle of WUFD, we should have clarity in our head and warmth in the Dahn-Jon, two inches beneath the navel. But when we get angry or have an ill feeling, the flow of Ki-energy is reversed, and as a result, the warm Ki-energy stored in the Dahn-Jon goes up to the head. Then, we have a headache, fever, dry mouth and eventually indigestion if the condition persists. To become healthy, we need to accumulate our Physical Energy, purify our Emotional Energy, and light up our Spiritual Energy. Health has its root in Physical Energy. So they say, with filled-up Physical Energy we feel less desire for sexual contact, with purified Emotional Energy, less desire for food, and with lit-up Spiritual Energy, less desire for sleep.

Most of us think those full of Physical Energy have a craving for sexuality. But the Truth is those with low Physical Energy lust for sexual contact. For those with sufficient Physical Energy, the thought of sex arises less often. This is different from loving someone. With purified Emotional Energy, we have less desire for foods. The highly advanced in practice can go for ten, twenty, thirty, even forty days without food. With illuminated Spiritual Energy, we have less desire for sleep.

The purpose of Dahnhak Practice is to get Physical Energy filled up, Emotional Energy purified and Spiritual Energy lit up. Without getting Physical Energy filled up, Emotional Energy can't be purified, and without getting Emotional Energy purified, Spiritual Energy can never be lit up.

The great Zen Master and Saint Boddhi-Dharma[7] wrote a book on how to develop in martial arts and I'll tell you an interesting story about it. When Saint Boddhi-Dharma taught his students, the condition to take the meditation course was to be filled up with Physical Energy. So he designed a practice called penis training. Of course, the practice was not for having pleasure with girls, but for training the students'

---

7) Boddhi-Dharma is the founder of the Chinese Zen Buddhism. He taught the students to get the cosmic Law not from the doctrines but from seeing one's mind.

Physical Energy. If their Physical Energy was weak, or if they were low in stamina, he didn't let those students meditate. He thought no one could possibly learn and benefit from meditation if their Physical Energy was low. He considered low Physical Energy only incurred sleepiness. In this case, Saint Boddhi-Dharma put the prerequisite of spiritual practice in filled-up Physical Energy.

Love which springs from filled-up Physical Energy is compassion. But those with low Physical Energy only seek jealousy. The loftiest love is compassion.

With purified Emotional Energy, we get to absorb the celestial energy, and thus feel no discomfort even with just half of normal food intake, or two meals a day, or even a meal a day for advanced practitioners. Also, with illuminated Spiritual Energy, a sleep of two or three hours will suffice.

Steady practice of Dahn-Jon Breathing will get our Physical Energy filled up, that of Dahn Martial Arts (Dahn-Gong) will get our Emotional Energy purified, and that of meditation will get our Spiritual Energy lit up. The basics of all these are Dahn-Jon Breathing.

Dahnhak has its purpose in producing a perfected person. Perfected people aren't those who create wind out of nothing, draw up clouds, or walk to a faraway place in a short time, but are those whose Divinity is lit up. Why do you think the Roman Empire, once so prosperous, collapsed? Parents are usually delighted if their children eat well. But they begin to worry if they become obese from overeating. When obesity continues for a while, all kinds of disorders related to aging begin to surface such as diabetes and hypertension. Their body's getting big but they end up with a short life. Amidst abundance of materials, but without the suitable spiritual development to go with that, the Roman Empire eventually perished. When people are preoccupied with the fulfillment of sensory desires, the Divinity, the right sovereign of people, begins to become indignant.

I'm worried about the health of humanity. I think it is vital for us to move at once from the culture of materials to that of seeking spiritual affluence. To miss the time for that will have a grave consequence on society. Before we get too obese, we need to control our weight with proper exercise. Once we put on too much weight, it's really hard to take off fat. Likewise, when we are rotten to the core materially, no philosophy or ideology will be fit for helping us. So before we start on Dahn-Jon Breathing, we need to consolidate, on our own, those principles I've mentioned; The Principle of Health, that of WUFD and that of PEA-EEP-SEL.

To move away from the Principle of Life is destructive. This happened during Korean War. A mother was on the road seeking refuge with her young son. They hadn't eaten for several days, and were starving to death. Suddenly, they ran into a sweet potato field. The mother was extremely moral. So she tried to find the owner to get permission to eat some sweet potatoes, but in the midst of war, the owner was nowhere to be found. Now, the mother had two choices: the first was to put morality in the supreme, and let the child die without eating the sweet potatoes, while the second was the mother's thought was flexible enough to eat sweet potatoes to save life and later, if the circumstances allow, pay back to the owner. The first was to kill human life and the second was to steal. Which choice was wiser? The second choice has the Principle of Life, regarding the life as the most important. Problems arise when we get out of this Principle of Life. Eating to become healthy is beautiful.

The social ills of modern society lie in the fact that sound common sense is not established. The reason that sound common sense couldn't take roots can be found in the conflicting influences of various philosophies, religions and ideologies. This society can be healthy only when sound common sense can take firm roots.

Precepts come in response to the needs of the period; therefore, no percept is perfect. To be equipped with sound common sense, we need to contemplate and practice. Common sense is more advanced than the logical reasoning. But, there are more advanced standards, and that is to see if they're beneficial or not when applied to the reality. At least if we are an adult over eighteen years old, we need to establish the Principle of Health: the principle of individual health, that of social health, that of national health, and that of humanity health. Now, that is common sense.

We need to meet the desire to possess and also the need of our Divinity. Only when we satisfy the Divinity, can we have complete happiness and satisfaction. I have Divinity and so do you. Where does Cosmic Energy come from? It comes from Divinity. People have the Divinity of people, and the cosmos has the Divinity of the cosmos. People are just a mass of energy originated from Cosmic Divinity. The Divinity of people always longs to meet with the Cosmic Divinity. The moment our Divinity meets and merges into the Cosmic Divinity through Dahnhak Practice, enlightenment will happen.

A person is always in search of a worthwhile object. A child looks for mother, and when grown, he or she seeks the complete and absolute world. That could be called god, the Law of the cosmos or the true entity of life. People walk towards that.

The moment we become completely merged with the Divinity, we shed the shell of the physical body and go back to Divinity. To return to this Divinity is the purpose of Dahnhak. Our purpose is to cultivate our Divinity, and let it be one with the Cosmic Divinity. This is called Human Perfection.

Have you ever felt your Divinity? As we need to learn languages to understand others, so we need to open up the ears and eyes of our Divinity to be able to see the True Nature, and listen to the true voice of the cosmos. Dahnhak Practice lets our Physical Energy be filled, Emotional Energy purified, Spiritual Energy illuminated, and finally lets us meet with the Cosmic Divinity, the fountainhead of life in the cosmos.

Those who have never encountered with the Cosmic Divinity can only fall in animal love or a love of convenience satisfying self-interest and selfish desires. They can never reach complete love and compassion. Only those who have met with the Cosmic Divinity can give a true love and practice true virtues.

DAHNHAK PRACTICE LEADS US TO ROSO
(RETURN OF THE SOUL TO ITS ORIGIN)

I'd like to introduce you to the procedures of Dahnhak Practice. Dahnhak Practice has its purpose in AESA; attaining enlightenment and sharing this awareness with others (Sung-Tong-Kong-Wan). AESA can also mean ROSO, return of the soul to its origin.[8]

ROSO is chosen by the enlightened as a way to leave this material world. I will explain the process of ROSO in detail so that you could check for yourself how far you've gotten in your practice based on these standards.

I've been engaged in spreading Dahnhak for some time, but have revealed only a little part of it. So far, I've spoken from the level of Ki-energy. In the course of studying Dahnhak, we'll get to know Dahnhak is the root of faith, fundamentals of therapeutics, and basis of culture. In the middle of Dahnhak Practice, a certain bodily movement naturally comes out, which is called the Dahn Dance (Dahn-Mu), and

---

8) There are eleven different ways to express the purpose of Dahnhak. To learn more about these, please consult Appendix 4.

through this, we get to know the beginning of the dance. Spontaneous humming of some melodies occurs during our practice, and through this we'll understand the beginning of songs. Songs and dances are an art of profound subtleness; an expression of our Self happening through the working of Ki.

Dahnhak emphasizes PEA-EEP-SEL; Once Physical Energy accumulates, then Emotional Energy becomes pure, and then Spiritual Energy lights up (Jong-Chung, Ki-Jang, Shin-Myong). Lower Dahn-Jon is a field to cultivate Physical Energy, Middle Dahn-Jon is a field to cultivate Emotional Energy and Upper Dahn-Jon is a field to cultivate Spiritual Energy. In the beginning, we sow the seed of Physical Energy in the Lower Dahn-Jon and grow them to the full. Then purify our Emotional Energy in the Middle Dahn-Jon. After that, sow the seed of Spiritual Energy in the Upper Dahn-Jon and develop it into radiance: that is Dahnhak Practice. Therefore, Dahnhak is a study to systematically advance step by step from the bottom up.

I'd say Dahnhak Practice is the cream of the crop in accomplishing ROSO. In any study, a plan and final destination are needed. The final destination of Dahnhak is ROSO, and the study plan includes nine steps. The first step is Initial Awareness(1), next comes Determinate Awareness(2), Right Awareness(3), Bright Awareness(4), Holy Awareness(5), Non-thought Awareness(6), Brilliant Awareness(7), Command Awareness(8), and the last step is ROSO(9).

To practice Dahnhak, we should begin from the Initial

Awareness(1). Initial Awareness begins when we realize acutely the transience of the material world and embark on the seeking after Truth. People have Divinity and therefore can't possibly be satisfied with the comfort of food, clothing, and housing. A person has a soul, and it will merge with the cosmos if it is well developed. Our soul is the core of the spiritual world.

So to transfer from the material world to the spiritual world, we need to go through mental wandering and sprout the seed of seeking after the Truth. Genuine love of Truth doesn't come of itself, but comes to us when we cross the river of transience of the material world. Without crossing this river, and the settlement of basic human needs like food, clothing and housing, we can't begin to walk the path to be enlightened. Those, who try to walk the spiritual path without solving the problems of food, clothing and housing, are just trying to run away from the reality.

Some enter the step of Initial Awareness rather late in life. For example, the famous Zen Master Hyo-Bong was a judge at first. One day he misjudged a case and sentenced a death penalty to an innocent man. Later, when the real criminal was caught, the man had already been put to death. A person without a conscience would have consoled himself saying it could have happened to anyone on any day. But he could not bear wearing the judge's robe one more day. He was tormented between his conscience and his duty to support his family. Finally he made up his mind, entered Buddhist priesthood, and later became a great Zen master. When we go through this Initial Awareness step with sincerity and diligence, we surely can finish the next step, Determinate Awareness(2) successfully.

Determinate Awareness(2) is a step we arrive at after we finish wandering; we decidedly make aims for our life like "I take refuge in Buddhism," or "I take refuge in Dahnhak." It seems that people readily accept the modernized Dahnhak and dwell on the level of health improvement and stamina buildup. The spiritual practice in a real sense, however, can never come from that frame of mind. But when I start to talk about the right mental attitude, people just go away. I want you to try to understand how I've felt inside when I couldn't speak up what I really wanted to say.

The same is true of lifetime membership holders of Dahnhak. When they sign up for the lifetime membership applications, I just leave them alone. Then I watch them. I try to find if there are any lasting, steady flames among them, but I find only a small minority have such qualities. When we have a burning flame in our heart which will never die, this flame will eventually develop into one which will illuminate our True Nature brilliantly. Those without the flame, however feeble it may be, will come along if love and efforts are poured into them, but eventually they will quit in the middle. Determinate Awareness(2) means never changing to the end of life. If we set an aim in life today but change it tomorrow, that can't be called Determinate Awareness.

With Determinate Awareness, we hold our teacher in

highest regard. The bond of teacher and disciple is built with respect and never shaken for a lifetime. In our times, it is really hard to get a person of rightness and honesty. People are so many, but so few are right. That's why I just leave them alone and watch them after they do the lifetime members' pledge. Only those who have consolidated Determinate Awareness can receive the Nine-step Procedures for ROSO.

The third step, Right Awareness(3), brings right deeds. In this step, we need to earnestly study three departments: the study of practice, the study of living, and the rendering of services. As it is said that we need to practice like we have meals, we should practice regularly. We may skip meals but we should never forget to practice. Next, the study of living means to apply what we learned into our daily lives while not slipping back in practice. We need to adapt ourselves well to our daily lives.

In Buddhism, they shave their heads and go into the mountains; this is "practice away from society." Actually, "practice while making a living" is an even more difficult task. Some might have a false impression that it would be easier to practice while making a living, but on the contrary, it requires bigger resoluteness. It would have been far too easy to practice when we get away from it all. Nevertheless, practice away from society is not the right way. First, we need to practice earnestly, next, carry out the study of living with effort, and then, render services to follow our conscience. We can't possibly intend to be enlightened depending on the necessities of life from others. That's why we need to work hard.

To sit around in the temple in the mountain and pass on the Law while living on what the believers have brought is asking for trouble and far from proper practice. In Truth, the great Zen priests of Buddhism worked with their hands. They tilled the ground and farmed for themselves.

First, we need to practice as regularly as eating meals. Never skip it even a day. Second, we need to make a decent living by studying diligently in the study of living. The reason we need to make a decent living is to be able to render services. Third, we need to practice virtues discreetly through the act of rendering services. In rendering services, we need to "let our right hand not know what our left hand does." By this we can reach the state where the sense of honor is gone leaving no trace at all, which is the completion of Right Awareness.

Practice alone isn't enough. To retreat into the mountain and engage only in practice is not encouraged. For, practice is just like a plan when building a house. No matter how well we study the plan, a house can't be built without hammering. Likewise, through the study of living, accumulated negative actions are shattered away and new habits are formed.

Those bad habits we have formed in the past can be changed into good habits by the study of living and practice. In addition, when we keep having good results, we're making a good karma. Moreover, when all these are connected to rendering services, the trinity in the study of practice, living and rendering of services is realized from which genuine spiritual practice will develop.

When we have a resolution to persevere in these three departments of study, we are well under way to developing Right Awareness(3). On the other hand, if we can't put it into practice, though we want to, we're not even at the gate of Determinate Awareness(2). Once a resolution is made, we shouldn't be shaken from that, ever.

We shouldn't attempt to enter directly into Right Awareness(3), but rather begin from Initial Awareness(1) and build ourselves up taking our own time. "Am I seeking the Truth heart and soul? Am I feeling the transient nature of material world?" When we can give a firm answer to these questions, our Determinate Awareness is firmly established. At the step of Initial Awareness, draw up a resoluteness in seeking after Truth, then firmly establish Determinate Awareness, and only then, enter Right Awareness(3). That way, our study will be indomitable. We will have no setback. Otherwise, we'll go through ups and downs and can't even begin to think of entering Bright Awareness(4).

Through these processes, our study in Right Awareness is well under way and we can get into the study of Bright Awareness. Entering this step is called the "first enlightenment." Our actions are consistent with our speech.

Actually we can have a little taste of this first enlightenment even from a period of practice in the mountain. While we're practicing in the mountain, we feel there's no life and death, and all our desires and emotions have ceased.

But when we resume the worldly life and meet with all kinds of people, what we've accomplished within ourselves will tumble down. That happens because we haven't trained ourselves in the study of living. It's like playing tennis on the wall by ourselves is a world apart from having a game with a good player. Minding only practice can't be the same as practicing in the middle of living.

So the study of enlightenment in a mountain retreat is like taking one brief look at a picture and coming out. Genuine enlightenment comes only when we perfect ourselves in the study of living and the rendering of services.

The enlightened one naturally backs up words with actions. When we think we're enlightened but our action doesn't back it up, it means our study was carried out in words only. For example, when a novelist writes the words of god and some other saints, we can't say he or she is enlightened. Likewise, when we express the enlightenment in words, or have a false feeling of enlightenment, it still can't be called enlightenment.

The life of the Buddha showed the model of the enlightened person. He felt the transience of the material world to the bone. He had the security of having the position of a King, beautiful wife and loving son but still couldn't escape the feeling of vanity. How severe his inner suffering was to make him leave home and go on the way of seeking Truth! Initial Awareness is like that. He wandered around, tried starving or staying surrounded by the thorny plants. But the enlightenment was still far away. So he entered a snow-covered mountain but still was lost. About this time he entered the step of Determinate Awareness(2). "Because I have no teacher, I have to find the Truth by myself." He practiced again. "I will develop my soul. Who else but me can do the job?" He began to cultivate his soul on his own.

Then, "If I keep mortifying my body like this, I will surely die, and after my death, there would be no more enlightenment to pursue." Thinking that, he received a glass of milk from a shepherd passing by. How refreshing it was after starving for so long! He thought he could engage in sitting meditation then and looked at the sky while leaning against the Bodhi tree. A morning star was twinkling, and his soul absorbed the energy of that morning star in a flash in the state of tranquility and detachment. His soul grew up instantaneously. Then he uttered, "I am my own Lord throughout Heaven and Earth." It happened through the working of energy.

The teachers who had taught the Buddha were all yogis. The Buddha went into deliverance through his own effort and perseverance. After enlightenment, he worked up a great compassion that he couldn't keep this enlightenment just to himself. Buddhist scriptures don't go into detail about this, but he actually went through the steps of Bright Awareness(4), Holy Awareness(5), Non-thought Awareness(6), and Brilliant Awareness(7) at the time.

He had this great compassion to spread the light of Truth coming from the great True Nature. Supreme liberation from bondage or nirvana means going through Brilliant

Awareness(7) and then finally attaining ROSO(9), return of the soul to its origin.

ROSO isn't possible with the presence of body. Only when we get out of our body, can we attain ROSO. Dahnhak Practice requires the awakening be transferred to actions at once. Without the study of living, our awakening is no more than a fleeting glimpse of Truth. Then, we can explain Truth well because we have felt it, but it's not the same as the Truth we understood and attained by the study of living. In the study of living, we make a living which is the succession of actual day-to-day living. There's a proper way of living for each of the steps of Initial Awareness(1), Determinate Awareness(2), Right Awareness(3), and Bright Awareness(4).

At the step of Bright Awareness(4), we can have not only visions and enlightenment but also unusual abilities. Even among the high priests, abilities are vastly varied. Those on the step of Bright Awareness are not much different in their speeches and writings. Most of them explain and express everything. But they show significant difference in their abilities. In this step many practitioners surprise people around them with their abilities; many followers gather around those in Bright Awareness. Miracles happen.

When we go through Holy Awareness(5) and enter Non-thought Awareness(6), nothing shows outwardly. In this step, the abilities are hidden, and thoughts disappear. We are not even aware that we are in Holy or Non-thought Awareness. In Bright Awareness(4), bright light comes off our body and we look like people with extraordinary abilities even to the ordinary eye. But in Non-thought Awareness(6), even a ghost wouldn't recognize us. Some attain ROSO(9) at this step without going to Brilliant Awareness(7). Individual practice ends here.

Corruption will disappear in Non-thought Awareness(6). People can fall into corruption even in Holy Awareness(5). That's why we need to be on guard until we reach Non-thought Awareness. When we come out through that step, great light will be upon us, and with the aid of great compassion, we can enter Brilliant Awareness(7). We can recognize a right time for things, and based on it, we can decide if it's time to enter or exit this world. Then if we decide it's not the time to come out to this world, we can choose ROSO.

Beginning from the step of Non-thought Awareness(6), ROSO is possible. Isn't that interesting? In Bright Awareness(4), we can show our extraordinary abilities, but we have no idea about the way to ROSO. When we mature to the fullest in the step of Non-thought Awareness(6), we get to meet the Law of ROSO. When we refuse to attain ROSO at this time and come back to the world, reaching the step of Brilliant Awareness(7), we don't make miracles. We want to awake the world just with pure Law.

That Law is not to be received on account of abilities. Rather, it's shown to us and there's no more to it. What's really important is the development of the soul. So in the step of Brilliant Awareness(7), we cultivate the soul of others. When we see people, we only see the soul in them to decide if we can help it grow or not. What's crucial is what kind of frame of mind we have in practice. No matter how excellent we are in Ki practice, or how complete we are in Ki circulation, those alone don't hold much meaning.

Study of mind is possible regardless of our levels of awareness. It's possible whether we are on Initial Awareness(1) or Bright Awareness(4). Ki practice, too, is possible for anyone. But if we don't polish our mind, no matter how advanced we are in Ki study or abilities, the possibility for the development of our soul is close to zero.

So from the step of Bright Awareness(4) on, utmost care must be taken. This study is impossible without the conviction for Divinity. We'll just end up repeating Ki practice, dwelling on that level. I haven't talked about mind so far, not because I didn't want to but people would run away if I tried.

I myself went through these steps of Awareness thoroughly. Initial Awareness(1) began when I was a second grader in elementary school and continued on in my mental wandering until I had two children of my own. During that long time, I had some experiences related to Ki and heard the voice of inner consciousness. Then a tragic incident happened when I was an eighth grader. I talked a friend into going swimming in a reservoir who didn't feel up to it at all. The friend drowned and I was beaten by his father almost to death. If someone hadn't stopped him, I would have died. From that moment on, the question of "what's life and death?" haunted me. Books were no more my concern. My father, being an educator, was more at a loss. My mother had an idea. Paying more money, she let me room together with the best student. But he became a pessimist after three months with me. My roommate changed, and then, he too became a pessimist. So rumors spread among parents never to let their sons room together with me. Out of frustration, my father told me to stop the mockery of philosophy and first try to become a normal person. If I hadn't played sports then, I would have died. Singlemindedly I stuck to sports and earned third grade, black belt when I was in 12th grade. When I went to the Tae-Kwon-Do gym, students ran away from me or kept clear of me because they didn't want to compete with me.

I was always nervous and restless. During competition you can get hurt in a flash. So I was keenly alert and fought with a spirit of "win or die." The big lump of pain in my heart made me go until my opponent was knocked out. Eventually the head master begged me not to come any more. In the meantime my heart was in a complete wilderness. Only sports allowed me to go on. I put sacks of sand on each leg and worked my steam out until I dropped. When I sat quietly, the thought of my drowned friend haunted me and I couldn't bear it.

Endlessly I contemplated suicide. That's why I fought to the death if provoked.

Then I made up my mind to be right. I studied hard, went to college, got married and found a job. My relatives talked of me saying that I had made something of myself. Finally I became a normal man. Then one day, on my way to work, I happened to look into the sky, and all of a sudden, sorrows surged up from my heart, and I felt so alone. A sense of vanity wrapped me up: "What's the use of life if I keep living like this and then go one day?" My mental wandering set back. One day I was looking through some books in an old book store. I picked up a book and opened a page and there it was written: "Those who attained enlightenment through Dahnhak are unrivalled in the world." I felt like I had been electrified by a million volt. I experienced Ki, something similar to the one I felt when I was in second grade. More experiences came: during a workout, I experienced inner Ki which I had read in a book in the past but didn't quite understand. Though I was in third grade, black belt in Tae-Kwon-Do and had operated a martial arts gym myself for a while, it was then that I had a definite understanding of the meridian channels inside my body.

From then on, my life was led by Ki-energy. I was so immersed in the peaceful feeling that I walked slowly and carefully lest I let go of the feeling. I was very careful even when sleeping. Hearing the best time to prac-

tice was from 3 AM to 5 AM, I decided to get up at four, and my eyes were opened at four without fail. Once I got up, I went to a mountain. To be more exact, I wasn't going, but the energy led me to the mountains. While sitting, I saw a bright light in front of me. Later I found out the light actually came from me. I found sitting like that to be the most peaceful.

I quit the habit of getting together with friends for drinks after work. My wife at first welcomed this change because I came home early; I used to come after midnight before. Soon she was worried that I was becoming too quiet. She observed her husband going to the mountain early in the morning, just bringing some spring water and being off to work. Later I quit my job at the hospital and went to the mountain, which threw the whole house into confusion and panic.

After that, study got easier. While sitting down, a message came to me: "go to Mt. Mo-Ak-San!" So I went there. It was not like I saw things with my eyes or heard with my ears, but I was led by an unknown energy. Even in the mountain, there was a place I was drawn to go and sit. So I sat on a rock and went into deep meditation. When I opened my eyes, it was already evening. I lost track of time.

The long wandering from Initial Awareness(1) ended, and the study went on without a hitch. I went through Right Awareness(3) and then Bright Awareness(4). In the past I had lots of troubles and questions *in my mind. To search for the answer, I had read a myr-iad of books and had been to various places. Now, dur-ing my sitting, the questions I had before or the parts I didn't understand about the Bible and Buddhist scrip-tures were answered and clarified. I got to see the whole lives of Jesus and the Buddha. Basically the two lives were the same.*

When we sit in the place of Void, there's no life or death. I sometimes ask people, "What do you see this with?" Then they answer, "With eyes." That's correct.

We see things with eyes. They also speak of seeing things through touch. We want to see and touch the people we love. Then, is it true that we see things with eyes and touch with hands? No, it's not. To see things, we need to have a brain and a functioning nervous system to connect our eyes and hands to our brains. But, what's most important is the image: the last image we get to have in our brains. We live with images. When there's an image, it's life, and when the image is gone, it's death. It's the same as television. When the fuse is blown, it's off.

The only difference is if the image is on or off. Why, then, are we afraid of death? Because we think our eyes and body will rot and soon become worms. We have too many images. This is the world of consciousness.

In consciousness, there is an outer consciousness, inner consciousness and the unconscious. When we enter the place of the unconscious, what kind of images will we have? We transcend the concept of time and place. We can move through time, go back to the past or ahead to the future at will. There are so many phenomena which can't possibly be described by words. So when we try to explain, usually we say, "There is" or "There isn't."

The Buddha saw this. So he said, "What's in existence does not exist and what's not in existence does exist." Here most people who study by words are faced with a stone wall. How could it be possible that what's in existence does not exist? At present modern science can shed a light on this puzzle.

When we keep cutting down things and reach the level of molecules, they're not seen. While looking through a microscope, we keep cutting down and we reach an atom and finally, elementary particles. So we think there's nothing, but there's something to see to the trained eye. Likewise, something can be nothing to informed eyes. But, when there was no microscope, the consciousness of the Buddha looked through this. Not only the Buddha but many before the time of the Buddha knew of this. On the level of consciousness like they had, people can share information without personal contacts, through the process called "energy resonance."

They can make use of various energies in the cosmos and materialize them instantly. They can make a flower transcending all space and time. To be precise, they're not making it. They just make it to be seen because intrinsically it doesn't exist.

But when we get into Non-thought Awareness(6), we're not involved in those kinds of pastime anymore. We can enchant or delude people by pulling those tricks in Bright Awareness(4). It's sort of deceiving, but people don't know they are tricked. It's a story of another level. But if we insist there's something when there's nothing, we get to make the other a fool.

For example, you lent some money to a person, say, Jack. Jack hasn't paid you back, but three people claim they saw Jack returning the money to you. What would you do? You have been wronged and feel bitterness. But there's nothing you can do. After some time, even you get to think you might have received it. Three people insist they have seen it for sure. Finally, you think again, "I could be wrong. He could have paid me back."

The feelings and images we have are transient or incomplete like this example. Then, when does our soul begin to grow? This is critical. Our soul begins to grow from the step of Bright Awareness(4). It starts to develop from Bright Awareness and blossoms into maturity in Brilliant Awareness(7). Even at the step of Non-thought Awareness(6), where we forget our own merits and depart from attachment, our soul can attain ROSO.

The enlightenment talked about in Buddhism means the various states of awakening from Bright Awareness(4) up to Brilliant Awareness(7). My purpose is only at ROSO. The purpose of Dahnhak Practitioners is at ROSO. An organization should be created for those whose purpose of life is

ROSO.

An important role for adults to play is to help children attain Human Perfection. A child needs to be educated at home beginning from early in life. That way true parents should be born. I've paid so much attention to the education of people that I neglected the role of true parenting of my children. So these days I play the role of, sort of, Dahn Center Director at home. I've recovered the place of father.

Who should educate our children? True education is only possible with true love. At present our society lacks true parents and true grandparents. A grandfather can be a true grandfather when he can say, "This is how we get old," while getting old. A grandmother can be a true grandmother when she can say, "Look! This is how we die," when she dies. Only then will the problem of aging be solved.

We need to spread a movement for that. When the purpose of all lives is of the same, and people can give and show a clear purpose of life, the problems of this world will be solved. The basic problem lies in the difference in purpose.

Today I visited a person in a hospital. I felt his pulse and found ten of Twelve Symmetrical Meridian Channels were already blocked. So I taught him how to die in comfort. Inherently we're supposed to command our life at our will. We can take control of car keys. Why, then, can't we take control of our own life? It is foolish to say that stopping one's life is a sin. To be born was out of our power but we need to be in control when dying. If we decide that to extend our life further wouldn't help with ROSO, then we can stop living. Our mind wouldn't get clearer in pains. Then, what good would it be to die a few days later? When our judgment is like that, we should be able to stop our heart. If we have a conviction about the world after death, we can go. If not, we can't go because we are full of insecurity.

My body is not me, but is mine. Then it should be proper to have my body at my own disposal. We need to be free to this extent, and we can reach this step with steady practice. While we're diligent in practice, we'll get there over time. We'll be awakened to the Truth with conviction.

To be enlightened is the best. To see it myself is the best. But If we can't see it ourselves, we can still follow the teacher with conviction. That's what the teacher is for. We've met a teacher through an unknown cause. We need to have a firm conviction that we can get to where our teacher dwells.

An Energy Line will come down to us, if called and make us peaceful. We'll have true peace of mind. In fact the most peaceful thing is that our soul is flown away. Once we find out about that world, we don't want to live in this physical world any more. That's why it's really hard to cut off the temptation to attain ROSO in Non-thought Awareness. For, we get to know too peaceful a world, and see where the energy which directs us has come from, and see that the teacher has been connected to us in previous lives extending through time and space.

The procedure of ROSO should definitely include Initial Awareness(1), Determinate Awareness(2), and Right Awareness(3). We need to cleanse the residue of our past deeds. Sticking to the practice in sitting postures isn't good enough. While rendering services to this world, we'll be united with Spiritual Energy of the cosmos one moment. Until then, we should keep persevering with conviction.

HUMAN PERFECTION CONSISTS OF THREE STEPS:

PHYSICAL PERFECTION, SPIRITUAL PERFECTION AND ROSO

We are travelling on board this planet earth. We are sitting on the earth revolving in space. But our senses cannot feel that. The cosmos doesn't seem to be moving but it actually is. Since the earth was created, humankind appeared and civilization developed. At first, Heaven and Earth were formed, and then, through the harmony of Heaven and Earth, all beings grew and humans were born.

There's a saying that Heaven and Earth are our parents. It means all beings were produced through the harmony of Heaven and Earth. So we have called the Heaven father and the Earth mother from time immemorial. Likewise, a child was born through the harmony of a father and mother. As children grow, they can live on their own independent of their parents.

Human beings are called the lord of all beings. They were produced by the harmony of Heaven and Earth, and they are brought up by Heaven and Earth. But the current direction of development in human civilization seems dangerous when seen from the world of life and the world of mystic power which harmonizes Heaven, Earth and humans from a place that isn't seen and heard by people.

Right now, our planet earth is ailing. From the perspective of the Principle of Harmony, people are like cancer cells on earth. Cancer spreads when a cell disregards existing orders, multiplies infinitely, giving a fundamental harm to the life as a whole. Then the cell is called cancerous. Likewise, a person inflates his or her desires endlessly, through which the Principle of Life is destroyed boundlessly seen from the perspective of health on the earth or cosmos.

The wave of liberalization in democracy has brought in free pursuit of desires, and as a result, all kinds of unwholesome situations cropped up. The crisis on our planet is shown through cancer, AIDS, nuclear arms and chemical weapons. When people blindly pursue selfish desires as they do now, destroying the Principle of Global Health and Universal Order, the Principle of Harmony will set on works on an immense scale. These works have already begun.

How, then, did these negative situations develop? The reason is we lost harmony. The way to bring harmony back is to unite the Heaven, Earth, and humans into one. At the heart of being in harmony with the cosmos is the Spirit of Cosmic Being. The very Spirit of Cosmic Being can save people in crisis. It also reclaims not only the proper way for people to live but also the health of planet earth which is faced with the crisis of destruction. The Spirit of Cosmic Being is the highest Principle, and only this can prevent the whole destruction of humanity.

Therefore, the great reformation of human consciousness is imminent. Right now the value system of life is dismantled, and people feel the crisis closing in on them. People are in the swamp of inner turmoil and conflicts regardless of wealth and learning. We are standing at a critical turning point to decide if we get another millennium of peace or face the end here. Many people need to change their consciousness, but change with what? The answer is the Principle of Harmony.

What is the Principle of Harmony? It is the self-healing qualities in our body, the self-purifying capacity in the planet earth and Principle of Harmony in the cosmos. AIDS is a disease in which self-healing abilities are lost. Though not seen to us, billions of germs swarm around us. Nonetheless, we are doing fine without getting sick all because our body is equipped with self-healing abilities. But if we lose these self-healing abilities, even an invasion of a few germs would hurt us, making us helpless.

Our earth has lost a big portion of its self-purifying powers. So the Principle of Harmony has appeared to the heads of those with insight and given them a message. The Principle of Harmony also has given a warning to humanity on earth and shown the way for survival. How, then, can we understand the Principle of Harmony? It can't be transmitted by theories or scriptures, but only by Cosmic Energy. So I have the mission to let you know the Principle of Harmony and here I am.

First, let us take a look at our body. When our body

loses harmony or balance, it gets sick. Our body consists of harmony among Physical Energy, Emotional Energy and Spiritual Energy. When this harmony is broken, anxiety keeps piling up, and then, we have a headache, pounding heart, and indigestion; or we can go back and forth between constipation and diarrhea. Next, we can develop neuralgia, hypertension and diabetes. Like this, ninety percent of the illnesses we know of are psychogenic, meaning the disease has come from our mind. Psychogenic illnesses happen from the breaking of harmony among Physical Energy, Emotional Energy and Spiritual Energy.

The Principle of Harmony is the Principle of Life. Death entails the destruction of the Principle of Harmony. This applies not only to our body but to our family. When the harmony of family is lost, couples get into conflicts. When the harmony between parents and children is broken, family will dissolve. When Heaven and Earth are not in harmony, thunder and lightening break out; likewise, when the mother and father are not in harmony, fighting with each other, a hush falls on the children. The children stay mostly out of home, and wouldn't want to come home. When the harmony of a family is broken, however, the problem doesn't end there. Children can become troublemakers in society. They could become involved in robbery or other worse crimes.

Society is restless, and that restless energy makes everyone rushed and anxious. Also the sense of anxiety goes over the national borders and is transmitted to other countries. This pervading restlessness in the air produces a number of patients who, in turn, fill up our hospitals.

In the old days, people got sick mostly from ill nutrition or germs. Now, most illnesses are psychogenic, and therefore we need to clarify the definite cause of these illnesses. Most people believe in feelings saying, "I feel good" or "I feel bad." The feelings are controlled by Ki-energy which is controlled by the soul in turn. In other words, our soul regulates our Ki-energy. Therefore, psychogenic illnesses come from the ailing soul. But doctors have no idea about the causes. Modern medicine is dark in the area of soul.

Our world consists of the visible and the invisible. This cosmos is composed of the visible and the invisible: Heaven is invisible while Earth is visible. In our body, the invisible part is the mind, spirit and soul.

We did a host of research on the visible body. When something's wrong in a certain part, we're told what to do and what not to eat. But no study was done about the way to develop and train the soul which rules and controls the body.

At first, people put in all their efforts and took advantage of all the sciences on solving the problem of bread, the problem of making a living. Next, people lived for the sake of fame, power and money. Now people begin to seriously contemplate what the truly precious values of life are. They become interested in true value. I'm talking about the Principle of Harmony because it's time to let you know that. To realize the harmony in our body, first we need to deal with the problem of soul, the invisible. Next, there's a way to develop the soul, which is the Principle of Harmony.

There are a great number of ideologies and religions. But the fundamental principle is one; the Principle of Harmony. From the Principle of Harmony, the Spirit of Cosmic Being has developed, from which the Spirit of "New-Human/Harmonious-World" has grown. What is a New Human? He or She is an individual who gives out services and values as much as possible not only to other people but to other beings. New Human is the standard of Human Perfection. Once born, a person shouldn't live to just satisfy basic physical needs but also to broadly benefit other beings. Only that kind of person can open the Harmonious World, the world of Way and harmony.

Based on the Spirit of Cosmic Being, the world is one. The global community is one big family. It's not like, "You are you, and I am I," but according to the Buddhist expression, Heaven and Earth are of the same root. In other words, because this cosmos is from one root, we naturally pay attention to it. This is the same as the saying in Christianity, "Love your neighbor!"

So we need to recover the Spirit of New Human, and lay down a big framework to realize the world of harmony. If we neglect this job, the future of this world is only dark. The Spirit of New Human is corresponding to the spirit of Jesus and the Buddha. But great thought has no meaning if we just memorize it in our heads. This spirit of New Human is the very spirit we need to be awakened to or understand with our body. To be awakened is only possible by practice, not by knowledge. New Human is a model of Human Perfection, and Harmonious World is a model of Whole Perfection.

Today, I'll limit my talk to Human Perfection. What is this thing called Human Perfection? The topic of today's study is, "What is Human Perfection?" For, if this is clearly defined, the purpose of our life will be clearly set.

Level one of Human Perfection is Physical Perfection. Human Perfection isn't possible with a sick body. When I first began to spread Dahnhak, I only spoke of physical wellness, leaving out things like Human Perfection.

I said we needed to get healthy to become a normal person. No matter how exemplary a driver is, he or she cannot drive well in a car when its front tire is off. Likewise, if our body is ill, we cannot keep our mental health intact. So to make a healthy body, many fields of science including medicine have developed, and to provide for the whole, economics has developed. Economics has developed not to provide for one owner of a company but to provide for all.

People have a duty to feed themselves well. An individual has to be diligent and hard-working to support his or her body. Next, to maintain the respectability as a person, we need to wear clothing. Imagine a President, a priest or a monk standing naked in public. These would be the last people we would expect to engage in such activities. The same would be true of me. Just think of me talking to you about the Way completely naked. How laughable!

Because people are affected by feelings and sensations,

they get a stronger impression from the outer shell of clothing than the inner core of substance. So clothes play an important role to ordinary people. That's why the clothing business is prosperous. In addition to the problems of feeding and clothing, there's a matter of sleeping. It won't be proper if we place our body anywhere to go to sleep. We need a house to put our body to bed.

We need the triad of food, clothes and shelter or that of Physical Energy, Emotional Energy and Spiritual Energy. This is called Perfection. The Perfection of level one is Physical Perfection, that is, to become healthy. Next step is to advance further and put our interest in the spiritual world.

Level two is in Spiritual Perfection. What's the purpose of it? To dwell our mind in the place to broadly benefit other beings or in the Spirit of New Human. It's the spirit of brotherhood and sisterhood.

What leads us to be able to help our neighbors? It is to realize and appreciate "you and I are not different but one." It is to be aware of these: "You and I are one," "If you don't feel good, I don't feel good either," "When you don't make decent living, I'm ill at ease" and "When you are ill, I'm ill."

If we don't have this spirit of regarding the Self and the other as the same, we can't broadly benefit other beings. Christianity teaches to love our neighbor like our own body. But this isn't something teachable. Rather, it is to be realized, based on the Spirit of Harmony, that our neighbor or the person next to us is the same as me: we are one. It should be felt.

Feelings don't come about because of memory. What we direly need is to evoke the Spirit of Harmony as a form of concrete sensation. This enables us to act. Therefore, the Spiritual Perfection is to put the Spirit of New Human into practice. This means to realize the Principle of Harmony inwardly.

What is the Principle of Harmony? The harmony is the fountainhead of all lives, the place of Void, the place of True Self and the place of Buddha in Buddhism. The place of harmony means the place of the absolute that creates all beings, and when we know that place, we're supposed to attain Human Perfection.

When we know the place of harmony, Spiritual Perfection is attained. How should a person strive to know the place of harmony? First of all, he or she needs to develop the body earnestly; the purpose of this is to allow our soul to grow. Only when our soul opens the eyes, can we see the place of harmony. This is Perfection at level two.

What is level three Perfection? It is to see and realize the place of harmony clearly, and actualize the Spirit of New Human. For example, if we just watch tennis games but never practice it for ourselves, we'll never be able to play tennis. Once we learn how to play tennis, we should pour our efforts in practice to be able to be recognized as a player. Likewise, when we know the Principle of Harmony and actualize the Spirit of New Human, we'll be regarded as a perfected person. Then, it's about time you might ask, "What do I get from Human Perfection?"

There's an expression that soul flies and scatters away at death. Where does the flying soul go? Shouldn't it be the place where it's from, the place of True Nature? The two kinds of Perfection I explained before, the Physical and Spiritual Perfection, are the prerequisites for the human soul to be reborn after being perfected.

Those who know of it greet death as a birth of soul. But those who are ignorant of this take death as a dreadful thing which is dark and lonely. The death of physical body is the birth of soul. We have only a vague idea about soul. But the understanding of this is necessary in the aspect of Human Perfection.

A clear definition needs to be laid down. You are listening to a tremendously valuable lecture. If you are truly interested in Human Perfection, you need to clean your ears and listen up. You shouldn't let this get out of your mind.

Our soul is in our chest. When the soul leaves the chest, death comes. Soul has a firm hold of Ki-energy in the Middle Dahn-Jon; when soul leaves, Ki-energy scatters away. When Ki scatters away from our body, our body begins to rot rapidly. When the soul of a person keeps developing and merges into the cosmos at death, he or she attains ROSO. A person will reveal at death if he or she is really perfected or not. We can make many blunders in the course of living, but those who know the Principle of ROSO and strive diligently will surely attain ROSO, return of the soul to its origin.

A person who has actualized the Spirit of New Human is one who has understood the Principle of Harmony internally, and has helped other people externally. But there are people who have broadly benefitted others in trust of the saying that external practice of virtues will lead them to Paradise though they have no idea of the Principle of Harmony. Many religious people are often found in this category.

Those who have been awakened to the Principle of Harmony and have put the Spirit of New Human into practice will surely get an opportunity for ROSO. So Human Perfection consists of Physical Perfection, Spiritual Perfection, and Ultimate Perfection (ROSO).

The reason people live like there's no tomorrow is in their disbelief in ROSO and their ignorance of the Principle of ROSO. If people are given a sure way to live an eternal life, they'll do anything to live eternally. The matter of soul was discussed in the sphere of religion but not in the sphere of science. I want to establish the matter of soul as a field of science and make it known to everybody. Thus, I'm making the first attempt at it through this lecture.

You must wonder how I've discovered all these things I've been talking to you. I haven't read then in the books. No book in this world has told me about then. These are not attainable through knowledge, but rather attainable through diligent practice. We need to prepare ourselves to receive this profound Law and perceive this principle. This vast and supreme principle cannot be acquired by money. To receive the Law, I went through a period of asceticism an ordinary person wouldn't be able to endure.

We need to prepare our mind in three ways to receive

this Law. I'll tell you the three treasures; the quality of harmony or True Nature, the Principle of Harmony, and the teacher. Unless we truly believe in and cherish these three treasures, we can't get to the place of Human Perfection. To make a comparison in tennis, the three treasures for a tennis player are a racquet, the principle of tennis and the coach who teaches him how to play. Those who want to return to the place of True Nature need to believe in True Nature. They need to believe in the teacher who guides their journey to the place. As we should trust and follow the teacher at school, so we should, all the more, in the place of Law.

There are three kinds of aptitude in the study of sprituality. While listening to my talk, I want you to make a judgement on yourself where you are standing. They are High Aptitude, Mid-aptitude and Low Aptitude.

The people of High Aptitude are able to tell right from wrong the moment they hear things, but going beyond this realization, they help others awake. They translate their understanding into action right away. They longingly have sought for this and matured to the fullest. Those of High Aptitude have a strong conviction. Their conviction is like an iron and thus never shaken. It manifests itself consistently in virtues and harmony. Also, they are humble under any circumstances and far from being conceitful. Their conviction in the Law and principles never changes no matter what may come.

The people of Mid-aptitude have lots of talent but no conviction. They think and analyze endlessly. When taught, they have a quick perception and a good takeoff. Overflowing with the discerning mind, they don't have the vaguest idea if they know something or not. They have no conviction in the Law, True Nature and teacher. They are very capable people from the standpoint of our world. Yet, they are the ones who wield the sword to those with conviction. For, they don't have conviction themselves.

The people of Low Aptitude don't know if the Law really exists or not. But once they have conviction, they believe with simple honesty. Because they have so strong a conviction, the power of that conviction carries them to the awakening.

So who do you think would find it easy to study this Practice?: the people of High Aptitude of course. For, those of High Aptitude have an awakening on the spot. Next in order is the people of Low Aptitude. For, they have a strong conviction. But, if the Low Aptitude become the Mid-aptitude by some mishap, they won't be helped at all. They destroy themselves and others too. They don't know what to do with themselves. So much talent, yet so little conviction. If we can't be in the High Aptitude, we may as well be in the Low Aptitude.

Also, there are two ways of study in this Practice: self-study and guided study. Guided study means to learn things while maintaining strong conviction in the True Nature, the Law and teacher. Try to learn things while hanging on the True Nature, Law and teacher, and we can reach the awakening. Self study is to explore ourselves inward. Practicing consistently, we need to have an understanding of the place of True Nature inwardly, and translate our understanding into action outwardly.

Therefore, study consists of self-study and guided study. We should never keep our head empty while depending only on what the teacher gives. Likewise, there are two aspects of New Human: to realize the Principle of Harmony inward with steady practice, and eagerly act outward.

The duty of a teacher is to check these two areas: teach the Law, lead and supervise. To see the True Nature at last is our own job. That's right. To enter the final destination of the place of True Nature is something we should do for ourselves. The coach just tells us of the principles and corrects us when we are wrong, and that's pretty much it. Therefore, the practitioners should put conviction in the highest place. The most valuable person is one with conviction.

Conviction in the Law and teacher is the root for the mind to enter the place of True Nature. With that frame of mind, practice wholeheartedly and you can get to the Ultimate Perfection of ROSO.

Whole Perfection, the Spirit of "New-Human/Harmonious-World"

Our body is steeped in Cosmic Energy and our head is occupied not only by knowledge but also by intrinsic Divinity which had existed before the coming of knowledge and ideas. Divinity is the sacred spirit we got from One Divinity or Cosmic Divinity. Before we had been born, beginning from the time when we had been inside our mother, this intrinsic Divinity had been wrapped up in multiple layers of various ideas, knowledge, and culture.

Our time is the battlefield of ideas and preconceived notions. Now is the time to shed the outer shell of ideas and bring up the True Nature: then all arguments about rights and wrongs will end. Now is the time to have our Divinity merged into the Divinity of Heaven and have our heart merged into the heart of Heaven: then we become New Humans. It's high time that New Humans acted to construct a Harmonious World. Even with the passage of history from time immemorial, the heart of Heaven remains unchanged and so do our True Nature and Divinity.

To establish "New-Human/Harmonious-World," let us

think about what a New Human is. To become a New Human, we need to be beneficial and give no harm for the establishment of a Harmonious World. The standards for this are to have our True Nature illuminated, to be ready for ROSO (return of the soul to its origin), or to attain Human Perfection.

To become a New Human, first we need to be healthy. When we are ill, we are a burden to others though we don't mean to be. For physical wellness, we must begin Dahnhak Practice when we are healthy so that we don't have to live with an ailing body.

Second, we need to have a conscience. A healthy body with the presence of a conscience is what we need. Then we have the basic qualifications to get married. There are some who wouldn't want to get married on purpose to fulfill a great cause. Nevertheless, we can say we have equipped ourselves with the basics when we are married. But to get married with an ill body is to sacrifice the spouse with our desires. It's unfair as well to the spouse if a person without conscience tries to get married. For, he or she might end up wronging the spouse with conducts such as beating, gambling and doing drugs.

Third, we need to develop abilities. For that, we need to be diligent to make a decent living. Basically we can make a living if we have health and conscience. But if we want to raise the quality of life, we need to be a person of ability. Each of us needs to be a hard-working, capable person.

Fourth, we need to be mature emotionally. Emotional

maturity lets us appreciate art and culture. Then we can live a cultured life. Cultured life doesn't necessarily come with lots of knowledge and money: rather, we need to have emotional richness. Those equipped with these four qualities can be said to be respectable at least as ordinary people.

Fifth, a person needs to be spiritual. His or her Divinity should be lit up. It needs to be connected to the Cosmic Divinity. We can become spiritual only by reading the mind of cosmos. To say "I read well of the mind of the one I love" isn't spiritual. To say "I read well of the mind of trees" isn't spiritual, either. Those who read the mind of cosmos are indeed spiritual.

Dahnhak is a practice to light up our conscience as brightly as a sun. With a bright conscience we can surely get to AESA; attaining enlightenment and sharing this awareness with others. Many hold doubt about this, but I assure you that if a person of a conscience practices singlemindedly, he or she can surely attain enlightenment.

Our practice, however, won't improve if we retreat into the mountains intending to cultivate our spiritual qualities. People should practice where people are living. Going away into the mountains won't help in any way. A person can only be perfected within society.

I have talked about god before. It's not a religious god, but rather a principle and Law. The Principle of cosmos is god. God is present in our body, too. The Principle of Health of our body is god. If we disregard the Principle of Health, that is, deny god in our body, we'll die.

The principle of cosmos is the Principle of Harmony, and that of love. The Principle of Harmony loves beauty as well. Because people have been created to take on a resemblance of Heaven, they love and seek the beautiful: when this is impossible for some reason, they have no choice but to turn to corruption. To stray far from conscience and Divinity is the corruption. Though all people seek happiness, individual happiness comes from satisfying the desire to possess, and whole happiness comes from satisfying the conscience.

Heaven looks for a person of conscience, develops the person, shows the person the mind of Heaven, and gives the person a mission. The person of mission will be accompanied by helpers according to the Principle of Harmony. After some time, an organization will be formed. But if a big organization happens to lose the conscience of Heaven, Heaven won't forgive it. If not in line with the Law, it will perish. That way, numerous countries which were prosperous at first went down later due to the corruption of the ruling class. The reason lies in the destruction of the mirror of conscience on which the mind of Heaven can be shown.

Some of the oldest organizations in the world are religious ones. Religions have sought after the highest good. But religions were too much bent on maintaining their organizations to keep their pure purpose and providence. So they lost their original purpose, and now many churches are almost empty.

People neglect seeking for the common benefit, but

make a frantic attempt to satisfy the desire to possess. Most of them just pray for good fortunes: "Please let my child pass the college entrance exam," "Please let my husband get better," "Please let us be rich," and so on. The fundamental purpose of religion is common good and satisfaction of conscience. Yet, many religions of our time seem to have degenerated into satisfying only the desire to possess, and have been lowered to become a tool to fulfill the desires of the selfish people.

Reading the general trend, we don't seem to be able to raise our hopes on politics, religions, or science. Heaven has blessed human abilities and let us enjoy the benefits. Yet, the tremendous development of science is not used to satisfy the common conscience, but to fulfill the interests and profits of limited individuals, groups, organizations, and nations.

When a nation, organization, group, and individual recover their conscience, they can utilize the available knowledge and spirituality for the common good of establishing a Harmonious World. Then, we can have a changed world.

Science will develop further in the future. Space technology will experience surging development, and the robots will free people from manual labor. That is one of the highest dreams of humankind. From the beginning, people wanted to make a living without labor. Of course, people want some amount of labor, not as a drudgery but as a pastime. Labor as a hobby is fun. It's like an exercise or sports. That kind of labor is outside the labor for the purpose of living.

People have intellectual and spiritual abilities. Science is an area where spiritual abilities have been manifested. Therefore, to become a person of ability, a person of great capacity, and a person of mission, we need to have both the intellectual and spiritual abilities; this is only possible when we have the right conscience. To go back to my original point of New Human, anybody can be a New Human with a right conscience. A New Human is a person with their True Nature lit up. Spiritual practice alone won't help us to become a New Human. We need to work to seek the common good. On the course of exerting ourselves to accomplish "New-Human/Harmonious-World," our True Nature will gradually brighten up. Crying out for New Human without moving an inch only makes our throat ache.

I can give you a plan of a house where you can have your True Nature brightened, but you need to build the house yourself. I see some people who ask me to build the house, too. When you help me, it is actually for the benefit of yourself because it is to translate the Spirit of "New-Human/Harmonious-World" into action. Human character develops not from living alone but from group life. To be awakened alone has nothing to do with the construction of a Harmonious World.

Enlightenment is considered genuine only when it can lead us to construct a Harmonious World. It's of no use to have enlightenment when it isn't facilitative for the construction of a Harmonious World. Therefore, the enlightenment which won't lead to common good has no meaning.

To the eye of True Nature, the true colors of those who stir up people in the name of democracy are shown. That's why we need to get involved with right mind when we join a cause or movement. We need to decide the following: "In the light of my conscience and my True Nature, am I being stirred up?" or "Is the path being pursued here facilitative in lighting up my True Nature and perfecting myself?" No matter how great a world we may build up, if we are asked to do it at the risk of ruining our moral integrity and character, it can be called a demagoguery. While individual morality is broken and noble character is tarnished, to cry out "for the sake of democracy!" is ridiculous.

For example, to throw a bottle grenade is bad. It has meant that the other party should die as a result of the bottle grenade. That's why each of us should be a New Human. With the right conscience, we can become spiritual. The path to the spiritual brightness is the study of Dahnhak: to understand the Cosmic Mind. Because "Cosmic Mind is my mind" and "Cosmic Energy is my energy," you and I are one. This is indeed natural. Most of us understand helping others as a sacrifice. When we live a life to satisfy our sacred conscience after the eyes of our True Nature have been opened, we'll naturally act in a way that "it's good for you and good for me, too"; this is in no way a sacrifice. Those who are awakened to the True Nature never make a sacrifice of themselves. All their actions are for themselves. But those who aren't awakened to the True Nature help others while sacrificing themselves. That's why they want to get back as much as they have sacrificed.

We'll have an era of the union of the god and person in time. The sacred energy will work to light up human Divinity. When people are liberated from the ideas and accustomed conceptions after their True Nature is lit up, they are said to be resurrected. Resurrection means none other than the liberation from the preconceived ideas. Enlightenment means none other than to become a person of mission for the purpose of accomplishing "New-Human/Harmonious-World." I haven't come forward to become a savior myself but to develop many spiritual guides. I don't mean to tell the world I'm a man of mission. Rather, I want to cultivate as many people of mission as possible.

Whether you are a person of mission or a helper, conscience is the most important. Intelligence can be a little in excess or in want. But there's a big worm eating away the conscience: it's self-justification. When we keep justifying ourselves, gradually our conscience gets smaller. When we drop the worm of self-justification, our conscience gets brighter, and our heart becomes so pure before Heaven: Heaven will cherish this pure heart. Heaven is ever so pure and dead earnest. That's why the four seasons come in correct order. The Law of cosmos won't play tricks. Therefore, Heaven chooses those who won't resort to the quick and easy answers of life. Even though we are lacking abilities, short of emotional qualities, or in a little want of spirituality, if we have the right conscience, we are loved by people and Heaven. Those kind of people will make this earth a Harmonious World.

At present I'm campaigning to revive the conscience. Dahnhak is a movement to enliven the conscience. It's important to love people, but to love Heaven is too beautiful to describe with words. We need to know Cosmic Energy and devote ourselves wholeheartedly in our love of Heaven. If we want to become a spiritual person, Heaven should pour out its soul to us. As we need to spare no pains to be loved by a person, so we should devote ourselves all the more to become spiritual people. Then Heaven will pour love on us, and only with the generous love of Heaven, can we become spiritual people.

What about our worldly love? Even in the case of relative love like this, we are happy when loved. Because our lovers are not eternal, however, we are happy one moment, and unhappy the next. When we don't feel we are being loved, we get jealous. Love even makes us involved in killing. But the love of Heaven is completely different. It's a continuous joy. People have the ability to be awakened at birth. When we keep going while unshaken in the conscience and conviction in our ability to be awakened, we can surely be enlightened, having our True Nature lit up. When we live being faithful to the purpose of "New-Human/Harmonious-World," we can have our True Nature lit up in the course of living. The degree of brightness may vary a little, but we sure can do it.

That's why organization is important. Within an organization which has a right purpose, we can develop ourselves while receiving the energy of the organization. On the other hand, when we join a gang or terrorist group, we will become criminals. Because a person is a social being, he or she can't live alone. Then, the kind of group or organization we choose to become involved in is of importance. We are affected by the purpose and atmosphere of the organization we're with. That's why a person is called a social being. When we join a good organization and work actively, we can get ahead without much difficulties and loneliness.

Also, I'm asking you not to rush into marriage. First, you need to become a New Human, and then, when you meet another New Human, you can get married. Only then, will your children be blessed and your family thrive. This wonderful world should see the birth of many families that broadly benefit other beings: you're the one to start it now. Devote yourself to become a New Human and meet the right partner. From now on, we need to have a family-centered society. There is no greater word than *mother* or *father*. President, doctors, scientists may be great, but no position is greater than that of a mother and father. A mother or father should become a spiritual guide and philosopher. So our children will absorb knowledge outside, but it is we, parents that pass them the proper spiritual life.

Our world is completely prepared to build a Harmonious World in the aspects of organization and technologies. When the UN and its associated organizations are fully functioning, we can be one big global community. Our times are the battleground of the conscientious and unconscientious forces. They are in a huge tug of war. What's scary is that because of the top-notch technologies, we can perish instantly if that's the outcome of these wars, or we can build a Harmonious World in an instant if that's the outcome. So without this campaign of reviving conscience, our earth can face the end.

Sacred conscience is the mind of cosmos. You have come to Dahn Centers to have that kind of mind. When we put our mind on "New-Human/Harmonious-World," and get the summons and mission from Heaven, Cosmic Energy will naturally fall down on us even when we don't sit for Dahn-Jon Breathing. On those occasions, devoting ourselves to our mission is the shortest way for our transformation. From actual works and achievements, our conscience can develop, not just from sitting and breathing.

That's why I've been telling you spreading Dahnhak is the very practice of Dahnhak. Individual practice is needed but to spread Dahnhak sooner is more important. Just sitting down and sticking to Dahn-Jon Breathing won't do because spiritual development and conscience cultivation won't come from practicing alone. Our character will be developed when we devote ourselves to the sacred causes like our campaign. That's why we have over 10,000 Dahnhak volunteer teachers who give free classes every morning in the public parks of South Korea. They are Dahnhak students like you, but they want to share with others the happier life they enjoy from this Practice.

I hope many of you come forward and say: "I've had

conviction in knowledge until today, but from now on, I'll devote myself for the cause of 'New-Human/Harmonious-World.' I'll live my life with all my heart." Ultimately we do all these for ourselves. So stay with us till the end with a firm conviction.

I feel sad when young people are in a state of mental wandering without a clear value system. To meet with a clear value system is like meeting with a good teacher. A good teacher's job is to spread the right ideas, principles, and values. If a mail carrier won't deliver letters, it's called delinquency of duty. So please don't neglect to tell what you know and feel in a clear manner. That's the way to become a beneficial person to attain "New-Human/Harmonious-World."

When we pray earnestly to Heaven that the sacred energy of Heaven will get firm hold of us, we can light up our sacred conscience. The mirror of bright conscience will reflect the world as it is. This way, our conscience will become bright and eternal, and Cosmic True Nature will light upon our True Nature with a pure energy. Then, we will pray that the sacred light and energy of the cosmos will immerse us, let us totally merged with it, dissolving us.

The heart of Heaven is the subject and we are the object. Let's concentrate our mind towards the subject. All laws of motion have a center. All beings revolve around the center. So we will concentrate all our heart on the heart of Heaven, our center, and unite our heart to that of Heaven. Between Heaven and us, we are the object, but between the world and us, we are the subject. Now, we've found the purpose and direction of our life: we've found an object for our passion, an eternal object for love.

I was overjoyed when I found the purpose of life and the object for love. It meant I could put a stop to mental wandering of 20 years. To resolve that anguish, I tried visiting temples, seeing sages, but none gave me an idea. Finally, I made up my mind to resolve it by myself and devoted myself to Heaven.

"I've found no teacher in this world. Please, Heaven! Be my teacher!" I stuck to Heaven which wasn't seen to my eyes or felt with my hands. "If you don't solve my anguish and suffering, life is meaningless and so I want to give my life back to you." I devoted all my time and energy with a pure heart. That way I realized the heart of Heaven and was awakened to the Truth by myself. Then I cried out: "my mind is Cosmic Mind, and my energy is Cosmic Energy." I was able to see this world from the place of Cosmic Mind.

I took great pains to design the means to spread this awakening. If I had tried to tell the heart of awakening at the start, nobody would have listened. So I made my first target on human desire to possess and said: "You can get better health with this," "Your illness will be overcome." After sometime I said: "Let's get over illness with Cosmic Energy, and save ourselves, our community, and the whole of humanity!"

Dahnhak is the way to enliven me, my community and the whole of humanity.

Since I got the mission from Heaven, I haven't had a carefree sleep even a single night. Those who have got what they want without difficulties don't know how to cherish them. At this moment, inside your body, thousands, tens of thousands, or billions of descendants of yours are there. Innumerable souls are crying out: "Father, what are you doing now? Mother, what are you doing now?"

I couldn't live one single day without knowing where I was from and where I was going. I felt mortified not knowing why I should live and what I should live for. When I read that a person could be awakened, with single-minded resolution, in three days for High Aptitude people, in seven days for Mid-aptitude people, and 21 days for Low Aptitude people, I wanted to try that myself because the anguish and resolution to resolve the anguish pierced my heart. But you, Dahnhak Practitioners, don't have to walk the same path of wilderness as I walked. This may sound harsh, but with your physical strength, you can't come even halfway at the practice I had done. Fast of short period is easy, but try sitting for about ten days without eating and sleeping. The reason you don't need to go through these ascetic practices is that you have met a teacher who can guide you.

Conscience is the primary concern. The conscience which tries to live in one way or another while justifying its distortedness is pitiful. What do you want to live for? I hope all of you will become invaluable for humanity, joining in building a Harmonious World.

UNDERSTANDING OUR INTERCONNECTEDNESS THROUGH KI-ENERGY

Our body has the visible and invisible parts. Among the visible are flesh, internal organs, bones and cells. The invisibles are Ki-energy, Spiritual Energy and mind. Dahnhak is a practice which allows us to feel the invisible. Ki-energy is surely present in our body. Because you have been convinced that Ki-energy exists, you are here at Dahn Center. In other words, we are aware that we have Ki-energy in our body. But there are not many people who can feel the actual presence of Ki-energy in their body.

Ki is an energy and magnetic force. It's also called power or strength. We all know Ki is important. Ki doesn't have any form, color or odor, but we know for sure it exists. The same is true of mind. It is not seen, has no form or weight, but we know it's with us.

There are two kinds of people in this world. Some believe in only the visible elements that are seen through their eyes, and others know there are the invisible elements even though they can't see them. The invisible controls the visible. Those who only accept the visible are greatly different from those who accept the world of Ki and mind though not seen.

The former live only for their body and to please their body; the latter not only have a conviction that the invisible world exists and controls the visible world, but also can actually feel and experience the invisible world in the course of their living. What made you come to the Dahn Center is your mind. Our body needs Ki. A body without Ki is a dead body.

Also, when we have a vigorous Ki but no mind, we become crazy. When we have a sound mind and vigorous Ki, we are normal. Therefore, we need both Ki-energy and mind. But without the awareness of Ki, we can't be aware of mind. Also, we can't discuss the Law of nature or Truth when we don't even know our body. We know very well, at least in theory, about the spirit, mind, enlightenment, Buddha nature, god, and life. But knowing them by words and letters is not satisfactory. We need to feel, experience and realize them directly.

Most of you who are here have felt and experienced Ki firsthand. But when you go out to the street and ask the passers-by if they know of Ki or have felt Ki, less than one out of a thousand will say "yes." Many will give you a rather strange stare. Getting the feel of Ki-energy is the same as understanding Ki, or being awakened to Ki. After we understand Ki, then we can make use of Ki. There are innumerable ways to make use of Ki: to heal, to concentrate, to settle down our mind, and to have a harmonious view of the world.

To make use of Ki, we need to understand what Ki is and who the right master of Ki is. The right master of Ki is none other than our mind. Our mind is also called Divinity because mind is an inherent one with which we can see things as they are without being influenced by our conceptions, thoughts and emotions. Divinity is a sacred spirit and the True Nature of life. To use Ki-energy, we need to have mind or Divinity. When you first come to Dahn Center, you hear, "Where there is mind, there is Ki." We need to realize not only Ki but also Divinity. The study of Dahnhak is understanding Ki, and in the course of understanding Ki, we get to be awakened to our Divinity.

Because Dahnhak is alive, many of Dahnhak Practitioners experience Ki during the first month, and begin to heal themselves in two or three months. It's because this study is directly connected with life itself. If a study brings us no change even after five or ten years, it has no energy. In other words, it is a dead study. Eating apples in pictures is like eating papers.

So far we've eaten lots of those apples in the pictures. That's why the awakening and Truth are still far away, and our body doesn't heal. When we eat real apples, our body absorbs the nutrition right away, and then we can see some parts of our life are improving. A practice is supposed to give us benefits in proportion to our efforts. The practices excluding Ki and Divinity are of no use. To understand Ki, we need to regain our Divinity: the first step is to understand Ki and the second step is to genuinely enjoy Ki. Genuinely enjoying Ki is called an aesthetic way of life.

Profound philosophy is packed in this aesthetic way of life. This philosophy is not intended for eating well and having fun. An aesthetic way of life is to enjoy life itself, the whole of life. To heartily enjoy life, you and I must be one. When I and the whole world, I and life, I and all beings in the cosmos become one, only then, can I enjoy life. So since time immemorial, saints and sages have consistently talked of the state of Non-Self, of complete selflessness, and of death and rebirth in this life. It is a immensely difficult task to do away with the idea of "me" or "Self." So some people think of this Self as an archenemy and want to kill or do away with it. For this purpose they exert themselves in caves, Zen centers, and meditation centers of various countries. But trying to kill Self is not the right way.

This small enclosure of Self will disappear like a melting snow when we get our Divinity or True Self back. Then, we will meet with an aesthetic way of life: we are joyful when things go well for our neighbors, we lend our support to make things easier for them, and we enjoy ourselves when we are satisfied with the result of our efforts. So an aesthetic way of life has the joy of the Buddha and Bodhisattvas.

Turning green with envy or feeling sore at others' success is wrong. In this kind of world, it is only too natural that we find violence, destruction and hatred prevailing all over. We don't want a world like that. We want a world in which everybody can be happy when others rise in the world.

We need to become a person who can be overjoyed at

others' success. The reason it is so difficult is that we think of Self and others as separate. When we close ourselves up, everybody else becomes others. As we think of all people as others, we feel resentment when they make success.

On the other hand, when I open myself up, everybody else is myself. Because everybody is me or Self, I have no other way but to rejoice if I make my way in life. Dahnhak Practice helps us experientially feel our interconnectedness through Ki-energy. When we are in touch with our Divinity, pure joy naturally bubbles up from within ourselves based on an awakening that I and all beings are one. This spontaneous joy of Dahnhak Practitioners is totally different from forced joy or painful pretense of good nature. Dahnhak is to understand Ki, get our Divinity back, and then genuinely enjoy ourselves. That will help us build a happier world. To build a happier world on earth requires an awakened mind.

Six thousand years ago, a saint said, "One Divinity resides in your head and sacred Cosmic Energy is steeped in your body and limbs." Those who understand Ki can feel the sacred Cosmic Energy. Those who have regained their Divinity will know in their heart that One Divinity resides in their heads. But those who haven't experientially felt Ki have no idea about this saying no matter how great scholars or religionists they are.

The saint also said: "We are One Grain in One Enclosure under One Divinity." I want you to have a deep contemplation about this. This saying holds the profound Principle of cosmos, the secret of my Self as a being, and the essential of all religions. This saying contains a profound riddle you should solve. Our Divinity is our mind.

This Divinity means the True Nature of us all, the reality of no beginning and no end, the origin of all beings as mentioned in the *Upanishads*, the Bible and Buddhist scriptures, the place where you and I enter and exit ceaselessly, and the vastly spacious mind without any borders or boundaries.

The enclosure literally means a fence. A house has an enclosure of a house, a nation has an enclosure of a nation, the earth has the enclosure of the earth, and the cosmos has the enclosure of cosmos. One Enclosure means an enclosure encompassing the whole. It means the whole is all in one enclosure.

Koreans have put this into action in their daily living knowingly or unknowingly. One of the examples is a memorial service to their ancestors. A memorial service, which they offer annually on the night of a close family member's death, is not meant to pay a simple tribute to their ancestors. It rather holds a deeper meaning and philosophy. It is a form of practical exercise to put profound spiritual principle into action. It is an exercise to become awakened to the essential nature of One Divinity and One Enclosure.

On the night of a memorial service, the family circle and relatives get together and make deep bows, while engraving in their heart that they are from one root, one ancestry. The root or ancestry here doesn't merely mean one's father or grandfather, but the very root which all their ancestors and beings in the cosmos are from. That root is One Divinity. Indeed this memorial service is an example of practice which has been directly applied to their daily living. How beautiful and modest they are when they make bows to their ancestors and the Heaven from which they have come, deepening their awareness that "I" and "the other" are from one root!

Making bows means to accept, understand and feel "the other" in depth. Through bows, we accept and receive Cosmic Energy, the vast One Divinity, taking off the small enclosure of Self. Making bows is indeed a way of practice to circulate Ki in our body, transform our blood and Physical Energy, leading to the awakening to our Divinity.

Let us think about the meaning of One Grain in the saying, "We are One Grain in One Enclosure under One Divinity." My being is a whole as well as "one." But this "one" is not a separate being, but "one" that is connected to the whole and "one" that breathes within the whole. Apart from the whole, "one" can't exist. Only when it's connected to the whole, can "one" be a being as a genuine "one."

The Buddha said: "Mind has no beginning and no end. Everyone has a mind, and a person who is awakened to the True Nature of mind is a Buddha. When you become a Buddha, there's no life or death, and those who are aware of this will get an eternal life." These words have made the Buddha revered as a saint.

Jesus talked of Heaven and god. "In the Lord, all people are brothers, the same Son and 'one.' So love your

enemy because he or she is not your enemy but yourself."
Confucius spoke of "the Way of Heaven." Lao-tzu said,
"From one comes two, and from two comes three, but even-
tually all go back to one."

All these words of saints can be expressed in one sen-
tence: "We are One Grain in One Enclosure under One
Divinity." When each of us exists as only one grain, we'll
have no idea of enclosure and Divinity. Then, everybody
else is "the other." Then we surround ourselves with walls,
walls of others. At first, we put up walls to be protected.
Then, because of these walls, the energy is blocked from circulation. Soon, we'll be inflicted with a multitude of diseases, living a life of long suffering. Have you ever seen a
child who is playing happily with a fresh energy wearing a
woeful face? Only a child with shrunken energy stays dispir-
ited in a dark corner.

Most of us live a confined life, and yet we deplore that
we have nobody to love or trust, and that there is neither
Truth nor life: all because we keep putting up fences around
ourselves. In the saying of "we are One Grain in One Enclosure under One Divinity," not only the thoughts of the Bible,
Buddhist scriptures, Lao-tzu but also the core of all philosophies are condensed. Also, the way to enliven me, my community and the whole of humanity is represented here.

THE PURPOSE OF DAHNHAK

We were born to this world through the Law. We were born in the midst of the Law, are living in the midst of the Law, and are breathing in the midst of the Law.

The Law is not that of this world, but that of the cosmos. We cannot get ourselves out of this Law even a single moment. We were born by the Law, and we are breathing by the Law of the cosmos; this Law is eternal regardless of the birth or death of each of us. That's why this Law is called Truth and life. We have come in the midst of the Law and will be gone in the midst of the Law.

To be awakened to this Law while we are living in this world is called AESA. AESA means that first, our True Nature meets and merges with the Cosmic True Nature, and next, we actively share this awareness with others. In a smaller sense, AESA means to feel our soul and experience boundless joy of it because the root of our soul is Cosmic True Nature.

A person's worth is decided according to his or her purpose of life. Most of us cannot give a confident answer when we are asked what the purpose of our life is. When all us clearly know the purpose of our life, and the reason why we were born in this world, this world will become happier and healthier.

The purpose of life for human beings is to know the Truth and Law, which is also called AESA. People who have the purpose of AESA do everything, even sleeping for the purpose of AESA. Indeed, AESA is the purpose of life for a human being to be born and live for in this world. I call those who live for this purpose Dahnhak Practitioners. Those who come to Dahn Centers without this kind of purpose, but just do breathing exercise are not practicing Dahnhak. If some say confidently that their purpose of life is AESA, their life is Dahnhak itself even though they may not come to Dahn Centers.

Most of us, however, put our purpose of life less on AESA than on desires. But desires are like bubbles. Even if some people may put their purpose of life on AESA, if they don't know the substance of AESA, their purpose is nothing but desires. They can't be said to do Dahnhak or actualize the Spirit of New Human.

To put the Spirit of New Human into practice, we need to have a clear purpose of life which is AESA. If we know what AESA is, we are about 90 percent done on the study. When we clearly know the purpose, we can proceed towards it.

For example, knowing the letters of Boston is different from knowing the real city of Boston. Also, to find the way to get to Boston, some go by the letters of Boston, while others go towards the real city of Boston. So many people are engaged in spiritual practice or strive to be enlightened, but all too many are lost while being bound by the letters. First of all, we should not be bound by the letters of AESA or be lured to the dazzling lights emanating from the letters. The substance of AESA is to know the Law.

I'm telling you to know the True Nature of human beings. But these words of mine are no more than words no matter how many times I try and try again. Sometimes, I feel frustrated because I cannot convey the whole of my enlightenment. But when you are advanced in study, my heart will have gotten across to you before you hear my words. For, the Law is always there.

The Law is not something that can be sought for with eyes, smelled with noses, heard with ears, or felt with hands. The Law should be perceived as a whole, but when we try to touch it, see it, hear it, and taste it, we are stuck with a part.

The time is nearing when we won't be bound by the letters of enlightenment, but feel it as a whole, instead. But then, those who are bound by the letters can be said to be near enlightenment because all they have to do is to break the letters and look inside.

Some people live only on instincts, while others live with lofty purposes and ideals only human beings can hold in their heart. Most people who have come to Dahn Centers want to solve either the problem of physical health or that of enlightenment. The problem of enlightenment itself is bound by the letters, too.

To walk the path of enlightenment, first, put your purpose of life on AESA. Next, try to feel the substance of AESA not by the words, but through your body. In your search for the Truth, you need to have a regular job to make a living. Because your purpose of life is on seeking the Truth, your job is only a means to AESA. In the same way, daily living is not the purpose, but the tools for AESA.

The history of humankind to this day has been that of domination. Domination resulted in the hierarchical structure of society. I'm proposing to spread a fresh ideal of "New Human," based on the horizontal concept of society where humans love one another because they have experientially felt the oneness of Self and others through their body. The Spirit of "New-Human/Harmonious-World" is a cause to build a world of Principle and Law. The meaning of Harmonious World is to build a world where everyone lives a happier, healthier life based on higher consciousness of harmony. It is a world where the harmony is realized, the Law is brightened, and the Principle is well understood.

Dahnhak is the shortcut to actualize Harmonious World. Our purpose is in actualizing Harmonious World. On the individual level, AESA is the purpose but on the whole level, Harmonious World is. So the AESA itself is not as important for each person. The purpose of Dahnhak is the world where AESA is realized, where the Spirit of New Human is put into practice, and where Harmonious World is realized. Thus, the enlightenment or AESA of an individual who has no regard of this purpose is gravely mistaken and has no meaning at all.

In our Dahnhak Practice, some of us say, "I'm not progressing in my practice." If we put our goal on five dollars, that's the best we can do. When we have a large purpose, harmony will naturally be with us. So the proper attitude during practice is: "Even when I know just a little, I'll give others as much." We should avoid the attitude that we'll give back only when we know enough or when we have a lot.

Too many people have walked the path to Truth only to fail and waste their time because they haven't understood the true meaning of AESA. Actually, AESA, New Human, and Harmonious World are a trinity. Each of them is not separate but has originated from one. If we want AESA without the purpose to build Harmonious World based on the Principle of New Human, we can't be said to have our intention on AESA. Also, to realize Harmonious World has nothing to do with material wealth or power. Blind chase after money and power only makes people paralyzed and confined, functioning as an impediment to the search of Truth. We need to study Ki earnestly. Study of Ki activates the Girdle Meridian Channel (Dae-Mak), the Conception & Governor Meridian Channels (Im-Mak, Doc-Mak). Ki study is important because it helps us cultivate self-control. When we keep ourselves away from personal attachment, maintaining the selfless attitude of "New-Human/Harmonious-World," we can keep our mental balance.

The study of Ki, then, will be done naturally. As long

as we keep attached to things, the study of Ki is difficult. The study of Ki and that of mind are not separate. What controls Ki is mind. Therefore, only when our mind is opened and liberated, will the study of Ki and mind follow. Also, this study is not done for others but for ourselves. Benefitting others is nothing but benefitting myself.

Even though our conviction is a little short, when we try to spread this to those around us, Cosmic Energy will come down on us. When you try it yourself, you'll know what I mean. This study is not meant to be done just from practice in sitting postures. Those who want to realize AESA through practice alone are like those who want to ride a bike without moving their body. To learn how to ride a bike, we need to get on the bike and skin our knees from many falls. To ride a bike can be compared to living a life in which we make harmony with other beings around us in our daily lives no matter how difficult it looks sometimes. Practice and living should go together.

LET US CREATE THE SPIRIT OF HUMANITY

Ki is like water. It comes in and goes out. Ill use of Ki
hurts our health. Filling ourselves up with Ki is important,
but making use of Ki is also important. So when some say
they experienced wellness after some period of practice but
have relapsed, they have made ill use of Ki for sure. I'd like
to talk about how we can manage and make good use of Ki.

Our body has Physical Energy, Emotional Energy and
Spiritual Energy. There's also an entity called mind which
we can't see, hear or touch. But this mind is the origin and
foundation that create everything.

When we eat foods, we take in terrestrial energy. We
eat this terrestrial energy through our mouth and breathe in
celestial energy through our nose. When this terrestrial energy and celestial energy meet in our body, they produce a
nucleus of Physical Energy. So Physical Energy is present
wherever there is life. Not only human beings but also animals and plants have it.

Emotional energy is supposed to flow. Above Emotional Energy, Spiritual Energy exists. Spiritual Energy means to

see things clearly as they are.

While we are at Dahnhak practice, we need to know what Physical Energy, Emotional Energy and Spiritual Energy are. Without the understanding of these, we can't make use of them. Those of you, who say you don't see any benefit after some due period of practice, fall into one of two categories: First, you were so low in Physical Energy from the start that you take some time in accumulating it. Second, you have accumulated enough Physical Energy, but you can't use Spiritual Energy effectively enough to focus your mind.

So to make a good use of Ki-energy, we need to not only accumulate Physical Energy but also light up our Spiritual Energy. Because Dahnhak is a fundamental Principle, it applies to everyone. Any of us can get well with Dahnhak Practice. Our Physical Energy will be filled up, Emotional Energy will be purified, and Spiritual Energy will be lit up. In addition to practice, we need to make use of our body. When there's nothing to do, or when we have no job even though our body is in good health, we suffer more than those who stay in bed due to illnesses. When our Spiritual Energy is lit up, we naturally want to work to fulfill the purpose of our life.

In every Principle of Movement, there is a purpose and center of attraction. When we want to use power, we can't exercise power without a direction. Likewise, we need to find out our direction or purpose in life. Without the purpose of PEA-EEP-SEL (Once Physical Energy accumulates, then Emotional Energy becomes pure, and then Spiritual Energy lights up), our Spiritual Energy will be darkened, Emotional Energy will become impure, and Physical Energy won't be produced. When we make our purpose in life right, we'll become brighter. Our worth as a human being is decided depending on how bright and right our purpose is. What our Spiritual Energy and Emotional energy are used for is important.

I want you to open your eyes wide. What kind of eyes will you open? True Self is not something that can be learned, but that will be realized when we get rid of our pre-conceived ideas and conceptions. Feeling bashful or awk-ward is the fence and bars that confine us. We all have the ability to hear the sound of nature. Our body is equipped with the talent to express beauty through it. We feel so awk-ward when we try to "express" this beauty. It's supposed to "be expressed" spontaneously.

When the art, martial arts, and music attain their high-est completion, their True Nature will appear. Deep in the unconscious, the genuine comes out. Those who have deep-ened in their practice of Dahnhak sometimes paint and find out, to their surprise, the painting is not what they have had in mind. They must have painted in the unconscious

Also, when a musician does Dahnhak Practice for some time, he or she leaps to a remarkable stage. A perfected artist isn't produced out of education, but out of instincts and True Nature. We need to get into the Non-Self state to do real art. The same applies to martial arts. None of these is possible if we haven't gotten rid of our preconceived ideas and conception. Only then, will we be led to complete freedom.

Most of us move our hands naturally to the parts of our body that are hurting. We rub and massage these parts. When we develop further from there, our hands spontaneously go to the parts of another's body that are hurting and ailing. This is the phenomenon happening in the basic developmental stage of Dahnhak Practice.

When we are pure and calm, we can perceive what the other wants to say before he or she actually starts to say anything. When we look at the other, we can perceive what he or she has in mind. Words or thoughts are manifestations of energy, and therefore, we can feel them intuitively.

But words are not perfect. Between the cash and checks we are using, words can be compared to checks. Real cash can be compared to our facial looks and Ki-energy. That's why our words are sometimes dishonored the same as checks are bounced. In this way, writings can be said to be a step worse than words. Only the words without words are genuine. Therefore, those who don't say any words don't lie. Because of the presence of words, genuine archetype of all existence is massively changed. When words are transferred into writings, more problems arise. But the complex nature of modern society has made us put more faith in words and writings. So we have too many dishonored words and writings. We need to be able to see Ki-energy, true meaning between the words and lines of the writings.

Then, what are sick people? Their Ki-energy is out of order. In other words their mind is out of order. These days doctors are not so successful in curing patients because they only see the body of the patient. While the body is controlled by the mind, doctors only see the body excluding mind. That's why we say Dahnhak is therapeutic, artistic and spiritual.

Would you rather learn Dahnhak from books? Mechanical memorization of the books won't help Dahnhak Practitioners. In fact, doing so is just like putting on more layers of paint. When you memorize the whole of the Bible, would you be someone who is closer to Jesus? For the same reason, the memorization of the Buddhist scriptures won't lead us to live a life like the Buddha. Still, too many people excessively believe in words and writings in our times.

When we stay next to a sick person for some time, we are likely to become sick too. When we are bound by writings and ideas, no matter how long we chew and eat, we can't absorb any nutrients. Which would you rather eat? Would you choose the letters of an apple or the pictures of an apple? Let's eat the real apples. For the wellbeing of our soul, we need to be in touch with Cosmic Truth. We need to keep absorbing the energy from the Cosmic Truth. There is a mirror and the sun. You are a mirror and the Cosmic Truth is the sun. Something is encompassing and covering the mirror. That something is your ideas and conceptions.

We didn't have any conceptions in the beginning. Later the currency changed, and we got to have personal checks, money orders and cashier's checks. Personal checks can be compared to writings. Still, people of our times take less account of living words than of documents and writings.

It's not hard for you to be a normal human being. Don't think you will be a sage or be in tune with the Law, but think that you'll be a normal person. Dahnhak is a study that helps you become a normal person. What I mean by "normal" is to polish off the layers of conceptions and regain the original pure state which we were born with and is represented by mind and True Nature.

Dahnhak has its purpose in making ourselves "normal." Therefore, we always need to see our mind to check if there are some impurities or not. As we keep polishing the tarnished mirror, so we need to polish our mind. Impurities mean our preconceived thoughts and conceptions. But, because these are not seen, we cannot polish them out with our hands. How, then, can we clean them? We'll just have to light up our Spiritual Energy. Next, we'll set up a clear purpose of life and then, make use of Ki and Spiritual Energy for our own purpose. We need to repeat this procedure continuously.

That's why we need the good maintenance of our energy. If we use too much energy, we'll be out of it. Then again, if we leave our energy unused, it will go stale and bad. I have been using some "checks" of my own in the hopes to let you understand the nucleus as soon as possible, but sometimes I feel impatient. How nice it would be if you can just perceive what I have in mind when you see me! I sincerely hope your soul will be lit up, shining radiant light upon this world.

The purpose of life is absolutely not in the accessories or conceptions. Students often ask if tests are everything in life. Fame, marriage, success can't be everything in life let alone tests. They are all outer shells and will come off in time. When all is come off, genuine essence is left. We need to stick with the genuine essence. Don't ever think of holding on to the fake.

Some understand what I say and others don't have any idea. Why do you not understand? Because you are too deeply wrapped up in conceptions and ideas. You show rejection to my words, becoming critical of me. What I say is not thoughts or conceptions. It is reality. So just try to receive it. Let your mind and heart open wide. Then you can be one with me in an instant.

I haven't learned Dahn-Jon Breathing from anyone, not even a single lesson. Through the workings of the mystic Way, what comes out through my mouth has become the methods. It's all possible because I saw the nucleus one day and had my mind brightened. I may even say it happened "suddenly one day." Of course I had spent long years persevering in inner turmoil before that happened. But since my Spiritual Energy lit up, I have said as I saw and felt.

I don't know how I would react myself. My hands may extend to one of the sick people who are here today. When your soul calls out for me, my hands spontaneously go towards you. But for that, your soul needs to long for the healing. If your thoughts want me to heal you, my hands won't move. I mean you need to be earnest. When an earnest energy is released from your body, my energy responds. I am always moving in stillness. I hope you'd understand that principle, too. There are thousands of methods to get to that principle, but as long as you cling to the methods themselves or you are bound by methods, you will never get to the Truth. Practice and study will help you attain that. So keep it up with perseverance.

I encourage you to read books, *Dahnhak* and *Dahnhak Practitioner* three times or more. These books will help you clear of the conceptions and ideas sooner. The more you read them, the deeper you will understand. No part of these books are copied from others' ideas or books. Rather, I have written these from my heart as the mystic Way guided me. When you keep reading these books, you'll be gradually freed from conceptions and realize why you are doing Dahnhak and what you should live your life for.

At first, you will read these books with preconceived ideas and conceptions of yours, but after two or three readings, most of you will be able to perceive what is meant. Your mind can be opened with no less than three readings, but you need to pour out your soul that much. Then, at the fourth reading, read it again with a fresh mind as if you saw it for the first time. Then your soul can be one with mine.

Let's be awakened to the oneness of our True Nature and Cosmic True Nature, and actualize the Spirit of "New-Human/Harmonious-World." The reason Dahnhak is spread does not lie in Human Perfection alone. At present, humanity doesn't have the Spirit of Humanity. A nation has the spirit of nation, a country has the spirit of country and a family has the spirit of family, but humanity doesn't have the Spirit of Humanity. We should create the Spirit of Humanity. I propose the Spirit of "New-Human/Harmonious-World" as the Spirit of Humanity.

About eighty percent of modern disease is psychogenic, which means there are that many wandering souls who are lost without any purpose of life. Even though we have the right Physical Energy, Emotional Energy, and Spiritual Energy, without a proper purpose, the order is broken; this and that is manifested in the sickness of our body. To be more precise, not 80 percent, but over 90 percent of people live without any idea of who they are.

To know who we are, our Spiritual Energy needs to be brightened, while we take multi-layers of conceptions off of ourselves. Most of us have become the slaves of our conceptions and ideas. Those conceptions should come off again and again, to reveal our true substance at last. Our conceptions are the collective whole of the education we have received, our habits, and social environments we have been in. I feel so much pity when I see some people leave after only a few months of Dahnhak Practice. They experience Jin-Dong[9] once or twice and think they have learned and practiced everything. The mystic ties have led them to prac-

---

9) Jin-Dong is a bodily shaking experienced by many Dahnhak Practitioners as the partially blocked meridian channels by stagnant energy are opened from the powerful influx of Ki-energy.

tice Dahnhak, and they just take off at the experience of bodily shaking. In fact, bodily shaking is just the beginning of Dahnhak Practice.

A wonderful world is ahead of us. I think probably those of you who are here today will be the forerunners leading the time. Therefore, I want each of you to regard yourself as an invaluable person. When you don't think of yourself as valuable, who would? Regain your spirit first, set up a right purpose of life and work with zeal to establish the Spirit of "New-Human/Harmonious-World" as the Spirit of Humanity.

What you learn in Dahnhak is not a conception. It lets your True Nature shine. I'd like to emphasize that you need to see things with sharp eyes. This Practice is deep and subtle. When we see that you and I are one and see the inner core, this world will become a Harmonious World, and a new order will be established.

With accessories dangling and things colored, the true substance is covered from the eyes. Seeing true substance is not possible by any religion or science. You and I need to be brightened to see the core of ourselves. The current situation can be compared to trying to tell peas from soy beans in the dark. Everybody claims his or her judgement is right. The moment the light comes on, we don't have to fight to the end shouting, "This must be a pea" or "I'm sure this is a soy bean."

Since we get to grab a bean only once in a long while, we stubbornly stick to our assertions. Some of us will even give our life because we think what we know is the Truth. Everybody claims we can have a faith in him or her. These happen because it's so dark. Science is straightforward in comparison to that. Science analyzes and tries to find common elements. So science will develop actively and lead people to see that their eyes and ears are not them but are theirs, and also, that these are nothing but the tools with which they can see the stars and hear the sounds.

These are very important words. They speak of life, and of true substance. This can't be understood by just listening to words, but rather should be felt in your heart. To do so, our Spiritual Energy should be lit up.

With bright Spiritual Energy, we have no anguish. When we are awakened to the principles, all our anguish will be gone. This kind of person is called a Dahnhak Practitioner or one who appreciates an aesthetic way of life. These Dahnhak Practitioners will create an enlightened culture in which the Spirit of Humanity is a common thread between people.

GLOSSARY

Acupressure point (Kyong-Hyol): The point in human body where Ki-energy stops over temporarily and then continues its journey along the meridian channel. When Ki circulation is blocked or stopped, it usually happens at one of the acupressure or energy points.

AESA (Sung-Tong-Kong-Wan): Attaining enlightenment and Sharing this Awareness with others. To merge one's True Nature with Cosmic True Nature and actively share this awareness with others as much as possible. The purpose of life for Dahnhak Practitioners.

Aesthetic way of life (Poong-Ryu-Do): To enjoy life itself, the whole of life. To heartily enjoy life, you and I must be one. The lifestyle of a Cosmic Being who has awakened to the ultimate oneness of Heaven, Earth and human.

Ascetic practice: Performing an intensive practice of self-denial and self-discipline for spiritual development and awakening. During ascetic practice, many practitioners go into a period of meditation and spiritual exercise without attending to the physical needs such as food, sleep and rest.

Celestial energy (Chon-Ki): The energy of Heaven. We usually get celestial energy through our breathing.

Conception Meridian Channel (Im-Mak): The energy channel beginning from the groin following the center of abdomen and chest to the chin. Consult Appendix 7 for its diagram.

Cosmic Being (Chon-Ji-In): A person who has realized the ultimate oneness of Heaven, Earth and Human. A Cosmic Being knows that the Void is the root of people and lives an aesthetic way of life.

Cosmic Energy (Chon-Ji-Ki-Un): The energy of harmonious cosmos. The highest level of energy experienced by the Practitioner.

Cosmic Mind (Chon-Ji-Ma-Um): The mind of Heaven and Earth. The Principle of Harmony.

Dahn-Gong (Dahn Martial Arts): A spontaneous martial arts that comes from strong flow of Ki-energy.

Dahnhak: A holistic health program which teaches people how to utilize Ki-energy. An individual first harmonizes the circulation of Ki-energy within the body and then, realizes that his or her Ki-energy is one with Cosmic Energy and his or her mind is Cosmic Mind. In this way, Dahnhak leads people to Human Perfection.

Dahnhak Practice: The methods of Dahnhak Practice include: Do-In Exercise, Ji-Gam Exercise, Hang-Gong, Un-Ki-Shim-Gong, Dahn-Mu and Dahn-Gong. Special training courses and Dahnhak Retreats are also available.

Dahnhak Practitioner: People who are engaged in Dahnhak Practice.

Dahn-Jon: The field of energy where energy is created, stored and regulated. There are three major Dahn-Jons. Consult Appendix 2 for more information.

    Lower Dahn-Jon: Located two inches beneath the navel. Physical Energy is generated and stored here.

    Middle Dahn-Jon: Located at the center of the breast bone. Emotional Energy is generated and stored here.

    Upper Dahn-Jon: Located between the eyebrows. Spiritual Energy is generated and stored here.

Dahn-Jon Breathing: A holistic meditative method of respiration to take vital Cosmic Energy into the body and accumulate it in the Dahn-Jon. Breathing is through the abdomen, not through the chest. The accumulated Ki-energy brings the peace of the mind and strengthens the natural healing power of the body.

Dahn Life Words: Short words in which the enlightenment and wisdom of Dahnhak are condensed. Consult Appendix 5 for an example.

Dahn Martial Arts: Consult Dahn-Gong.

Divinity: The quality of god, which is the Principle of Harmony and one's True Nature, that is present in all people. People are a mass of energy which has originated from Cosmic Divinity. Individual Divinity longs to meet with the Cosmic Divinity and become one with it. A person is enlightened when his or her Divinity merges with the Cosmic Divinity.

Earth: Earth embraces and grows all beings like Mother Nature. The mother of all beings.

Emotional Energy: There are three levels in the evolution of Ki-energy within human body. Emotional Energy is at the mid-level. It is created and stored in the Middle Dahn-Jon.

Energy Line: A figurative line of Ki-energy that connects the inner center of Dahnhak Practitioners to Heaven or Cosmic Mind. Through the help of an Energy Line, a practitioner can communicate with Heaven.

Girdle Meridian Channel (Dae-Mak): The energy channel around the waist beginning from the navel. Consult Appendix 7.

God: The god in Dahnhak is neither a religious god nor a personified being. The god in Dahnhak is the Principle of the cosmos, the Principle of Harmony, the Principle of Love.

Governor Meridian Channel (Doc-Mak): One of the three major meridian channels through which Ki-energy is circulated. It begins from the tail bone, follows the line of spine and ends at the top of head. Consult Appendix 7 for its diagram.

Harmonious World: One world based on the Spirit of Cosmic Being.

The global community is one big family. People in the Harmonious World know in their heart that Heaven and Earth are of the same root. Harmonious World has an enlightened culture in which the common atmosphere of the society is caring, accepting, magnanimous and spiritual.

Heaven: The Void. The Principle of Harmony. The father of all beings.

Human Perfection: The purpose of life for Dahnhak Practitioners. A human being grows his or her Divinity and merges into the Cosmic Divinity. Then, he or she can attain ROSO, return of the soul to its origin. The steps of Human Perfection are Physical Perfection, Spiritual Perfection, and Ultimate Perfection, which is ROSO.

Jong-Chung, Ki-Jang, Shin-Myong: Consult PEA-EEP-SEL.

Ji-Gam Exercise: A meditative exercise, which means in Korean, "detaching from outer consciousness of the five senses and going into the inner consciousness of the sixth sense," to introduce the awareness of Ki-energy through direct experience.

Ki-energy: The bio-energy or life force that pervades all beings and cosmos. In Dahnhak, where there is a mind, there is Ki-energy. Consult Appendix 1 for more information.

Law: The Principle of the cosmos. The nature of things. The Principle of Harmony.

Macrocosmic Energy Circuit (Dae-Ju-Chon): The state of supreme enlightenment. A step above the Microcosmic Energy Circuit. When one attains to the Macrocosmic Energy Circuit, one is completely merged into Cosmic True Nature and can freely enter and exit one's body.

Meridian channel (Kyong-Rak): The path of energy in human body which is composed of many energy or acupressure points. Meridian channels are spread all over the human body like veins. Important meridian channels for Dahnhak Practitioners are Girdle Meridian Channel (Dae-Mak), Conception Meridian Channel (Im-Mak), and Governor Meridian Channel (Doc-Mak).

Microcosmic Energy Circuit (So-Ju-Chon): In the aspect of Ki-energy, one can circulate Ki-energy to Girdle, Conception and Governor Meridian Channels and all other meridian channels in the body. In the aspect of breathing, one can breathe not only through the Dahn-Jon but also through the skin.

MKBP (Shim-Ki-Hyol-Jong): Where there is a mind, there is Ki-energy, and when enough Ki-energy accumulates, blood and Physical Energy are strengthened. One's level of consciousness determines the level, strength, and purity of Ki.

Mind: Mind in Dahnhak is an integrated whole of the reasoning mind and affective heart. Also, mind can mean our intrinsic mind on which things are reflected without being tarnished by our emotions and outer influences because "Cosmic Mind is my mind."

New Human: An individual who gives out services and values as much as possible not only to other people but to other beings. New Human is the standard of Human Perfection.

New-Human/Harmonious-World: A New Human is a person who has gotten out of his or her small Self. He or she is beneficial not only to other people but also to other beings such as animals and plants. Harmonious World is an ideal world where the Spirit of Cosmic Being is incorporated in daily living.

One Divinity: Cosmic Divinity. The True Nature and origin of all beings. The place where we enter and exit ceaselessly. The vastly spacious mind without any borders or boundaries.

PEA-EEP-SEL (Jong-Chung, Ki-Jang, Shin-Myong): Once Physical Energy accumulates, then Emotional Energy becomes pure, and then Spiritual Energy lights up. This principle holds the developmental process leading to Human Perfection. The evolution of Ki is directly connected with the evolution of the human consciousness.

Practice: The discipline or exercise to develop mind and awareness. Rigorous practice leads to the development of mind and meeting with the True Nature.

Principle of Harmony: The Principle that all beings in the cosmos need to be in harmony with one another and also with the cosmos. When one awakens to the Principle of Harmony, he or she realizes the interconnectedness of all beings. Harmony is the fountainhead of all lives, the place of Void, the place of True Self and the place of Buddha in Buddhism.

Sole Respiration: The breathing method of highly advanced practitioners. They breathe mostly through the energy points on the soles of their feet.

Su-Seung-Hwa-Kang: Consult WUFD.

Terrestrial energy (Ji-Ki): The energy of Earth. When people eat food, they are taking in terrestrial energy.

True Nature: The true entity or inner core of all beings. When human beings are awakened to their True Nature, they are called enlightened. The enlightened one will merge his or her True Nature with that of the cosmos.

Truth: The ultimate Truth of the cosmos. The enlightenment. The Principle of Harmony.

Way: Tao. The nature of things. The Law and Truth.

WUFD (Su-Sueng-Hwa-Kang): One of the three principles of Dahnhak practice. The cold of the water energy in the kidneys goes up toward the head and the heat of the fire energy in the heart comes down to the stomach area. This way, our stomach is warm and head is clear.

APPENDICES

APPENDIX 1

What is Ki

Ki-energy is present everywhere. It is the life force of all beings and the cosmos. The magnitude of Ki-energy ranges from weak as when we blink our eyes to strong as in lightening.

Ki-energy can be said to be pure or impure, and strong or weak. Ki-energy can be given and taken. For human beings, their mind affects the quality of Ki-energy they produce.

Much scientific and analytical research about Ki-energy has been conducted, but a full knowledge of it is yet to come. In 1939, a Russian electrician named Kirlian succeeded in taking pictures of bio-energy. His pictures clearly showed that sick leaves of plants showed a feeble aura of bioenergy, while healthy leaves showed a bright and strong aura. Also, his pictures showed human beings radiated various types of energy according to their emotional state.

In 1980, the Immune Research Center in Peking showed that Ki-energy can actually kill cancerous cells in a human body. The hospital in affiliation with Columbia University employed Ki therapy and confirmed that over 3,000 patients had received some benefit from it.

APPENDIX 2

Dahn-Jon System

Dahn-Jon functions as an energy center within the Ki circulation system of our body. "Dahn" means "Ki-energy," and "Jon" means a field. There are 365 acupressure points in our body, and these are connected by meridian channels. We can access and make use of Ki-energy by means of meridian channels, and the Dahn-Jon works as a storehouse and generator of Ki-energy. There are three major Dahn-Jons in Dahnhak. When we refer to Dahn-Jon, we usually mean the Lower Dahn-Jon.

1) Lower Dahn-Jon

Located two inches below the navel and two inches underneath this point. Physical Energy is generated and stored here.

2) Middle Dahn-Jon

Located at the center of the breast bone. Emotional Energy is generated and stored here.

3) Upper Dahn-Jon

Located between the eyebrows. Spiritual Energy is generated and stored here.

Three major Dahn-Jons

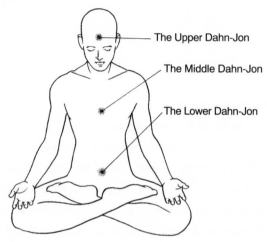

— The Upper Dahn-Jon

The Middle Dahn-Jon

The Lower Dahn-Jon

The Evolution of Ki-energy Within Human Body

According to the development of consciousness in human beings, the quality of Ki-energy evolves. As one moves to higher consciousness, Ki-energy gets purer accordingly. This process is called "Jong-Chung, Ki-Jang, Shin-Myong" or PEA-EEP-SEL; Once Physical Energy accumulates, then Emotional Energy becomes pure, and then Spiritual Energy lights up.

1) Physical Energy (Jong)

Ki-energy at the lowest level. The magnitude of Physical Energy indicates one's physical strength. Physical Energy is created and stored in the Lower Dahn-Jon. The color is red. When Physical Energy is filled up, one's sexual desire decreases.

2) Emotional Energy (Ki)

Ki-energy at the mid-level. Emotional Energy develops after Physical Energy is filled up. It is created and stored in the Middle Dahn-Jon. The color is golden. When Emotional Energy is pure, one's mind is opened and one's desire for food decreases.

3) Spiritual Energy (Shin)

Ki-energy at the highest level. Spiritual Energy develops after Emotional Energy is purified. It is created and stored in the Upper Dahn-Jon. The color is indigo. When Spiritual Energy is lit up, one's creativity increases, good judgement is cultivated, and one's desire for sleep decreases.

APPENDIX 3

The Developmental Steps of Dahnhak Practice

There are several ways to divide the steps of Dahnhak Practice. To facilitate the understanding of the lectures, some ways of classification are shown. The order of classification is from the lowest to the highest step.

1. The Developmental Steps According to the Breathing Methods

1) Dahn-Jon Breathing

To breathe in and out through the Lower Dahn-Jon. To be more precise, there's an energy point called Myong-Mun located on the back almost exactly opposite from the navel. Dahn-Jon Breathing means to breathe in and out through this Myong-Mun acupressure point with nearly no awareness of the nose. In Dahnhak, one does Dahn-Jon Breathing until one activates the Girdle Meridian Channel (Dae-Mak).

2) Skin Respiration

One mostly breathes through one's skin as a snake does. At this stage, one is said to have attained the Microcosmic Energy Circuit, which means one can freely circulate Ki-energy to and from any part of one's body.

3) Sole Respiration

One mostly breathes through the acupressure points on the soles of one's feet. At this stage, one freely enters and exits one's body. This stage is called Macrocosmic Energy Circuit, which means one is merged with Cosmic True Nature.

2. The Developmental Steps According to Ki-energy Use

1) Initiating

One feels Ki and is aware of the sensation of Ki-energy throughout one's body. One can get into inner consciousness. One feels relief of stress. Chronic fatigue and insomnia can be relieved.

2) Accumulating

One accumulates Ki-energy, developing Lower Dahn-Jon. One's confidence and positive thinking are stimulated. The function of all bodily parts is improved.

3) Controlling

The major energy channels of one's body are activated. Middle Dahn-Jon is developed. One's mind is open, and one feels peacefulness and joy. Self-healing power is maximized.

4) Commanding

All energy channels are activated; the Microcosmic Energy Circuit is attained. Upper Dahn-Jon is developed. One's creativity and latent potential are activated. The connection and union between body and mind are maximized. One's Ki-energy is purified. One will acquire healing abilities.

5) Completing

One is awakened to the ultimate oneness of Heaven, Earth and Human. Human Perfection and Macrocosmic Energy Circuit have been attained. One becomes merged with the cosmos.

3. The Developmental Steps According to One's Awareness

1) Initial Awareness

One feels the transience of the material world and decides to live for the development of one's soul.

2) Determinate Awareness

One makes up one's mind to dedicate one's life for the Human Perfection. But one's body is not under one's control yet.

3) Right Awareness

One's soul is revived. One acts right. One gets well on the way to the right practice.

4) Bright Awareness

One becomes bright. One knows the nature of things without the aid of knowledge. One can live a life according to the principle.

5) Holy Awareness

The prime of soul. One has unusual abilities. Miracles happen and people are surprised and attracted. People at this step still have the touch of desire to possess, desire for fame and pride.

6) Non-thought Awareness

One's soul is perfected. ROSO is possible. One never falls into corruption. One stays at the place of complete Nothingness.

7) Brilliant Awareness

Enlightenment in the truest sense. One, at this step, is called a saint. One has the mission to save the soul. One has the consciousness of Void, and that of cosmos. Great compassion is always present with him or her.

8) Command Awareness

Great wisdom is opened to save the world.

9) ROSO, return of the soul to its origin

One's soul is completely perfected and becomes one with the True Nature of the cosmos, original place of universal life.

APPENDIX 4

Eleven Different Ways to Express the Purpose of Dahnhak

The purpose of Dahnhak is Human Perfection and Whole Perfection. Human Perfection and Whole Perfection don't exist separately, but complement each other. Because Human Perfection can be expressed in ten different ways, here are eleven different ways to express the purpose of Dahnhak.

1) One attains to **Human Perfection.**

2) **Human Divinity** is lit up and becomes one with the **Cosmic Divinity.**

3) One becomes a **Cosmic Being** who realizes the ultimate oneness of Heaven, Earth and Human.

4) One's **soul** develops and becomes one with the **True Nature** of the cosmos.

5) **AESA:** One attains enlightenment on the personal level and strives hard to share this awareness with others.

6) One deeply realizes **Cosmic Energy** and **Cosmic Mind.**

7) **ROSO:** One's soul returns to its origin.

8) One becomes a **New Human.**

9) One maintains the **detached mind** from the worldly desires.

10) One stays peacefully in the world of **the unconscious.**

11) One knows the **Truth and Law.**

Five Requirements to Become a New Human

1) To have physical health.

2) To have a conscience.

3) To be capable.

4) To be emotionally rich

5) To be spiritual.

Three Principles of Dahnhak Practice

1) WUFD (Su-Seung-Hwa-Kang)

Water energy up, fire energy down. The cold of the water energy in the kidneys goes upward and the heat of the fire energy in the heart comes downward. That way, one's head keeps cool and one's stomach keeps warm. WUFD is needed for physical wellness. When we get stressed out or worry too much, fire energy goes upward, resulting in the reverse of WUFD.

2) PEA-EEP-SEL (Jong-Chung, Ki-Jang, Shin-Myong)

Once Physical Energy accumulates, then Emotional Energy becomes pure, and then Spiritual Energy lights up.

This principle shows the evolutionary process of Ki development. The evolution of Ki is directly connected with the evolution of the consciousness, of the mind and of the soul.

3) MKBP (Shim-Ki-Hyol-Jong)

Where there is a mind, there is Ki-energy, and when enough Ki-energy accumu-lates, blood and Physical Energy are strengthened. The quality of Ki is determined by one's mind. One's level of consciousness determines the level, strength, and purity of Ki. As one's practice advances, one can send Ki to any part of one's body. Also one can bring in the Ki from outside or send one's inner Ki-energy out to someone.

APPENDIX 5

Dahn Life Words: Enlightenment and Wisdom of Dahnhak

Dahn Life Words are short sentences in which the Grand Master Lee's awakening is condensed. Some examples are as follows.

1) Cosmic Energy is my energy, my energy is Cosmic Energy. Cosmic Mind is my mind, my mind is Cosmic Mind.
2) My body is not me, but is mine.
3) We are One Grain in One Enclosure under One Divinity.
4) One Divinity resides in my head and sacred Cosmic Energy is steeped in my body and limbs.
5) I am a Cosmic Being. I am Cosmic energy. I am Cosmic mind.

APPENDIX 6

Brain Waves and Human Consciousness

Brain waves	Cycles per second	Consciousness	Characteristics			
beta	13 & over	Outer consciousness	Consciousness of ordinary people			
alpha	8~12	Inner consciousness	*Consciousness of artists and some drunken people, *Visions of black & white	Dreams, habits	*Deep relaxation *Conscious -ness during Dahnhak Practice
delta	4~8		Visions of color		
theta	below 4	The unconscious	Cosmic Consciousness, Detached mind, Enlightenment		

APPENDIX 7

Diagrams of the Conception, Governor and Girdle Meridian Channels (Im-Mak, Doc-Mak, Dae-Mak)

Conception Meridian Channel (Im-Mak)

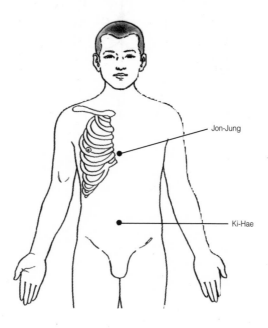

Jon-Jung

Ki-Hae

Governor Meridian Channel (Doc-Mak)

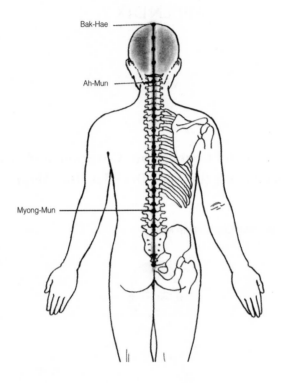

Bak-Hae

Ah-Mun

Myong-Mun

Girdle Meridian Channel (Dae-Mak)

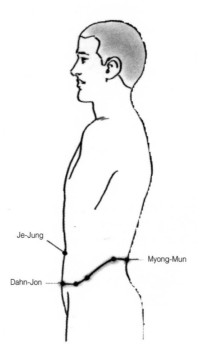

Je-Jung

Myong-Mun

Dahn-Jon